AN EDUCATION IN
HAPPINESS

©Ⓜ.ⓐ.ⓘⓝⓤⓡ
1916
Sir. Rabindranath Tagore

First published in Italian as
Un'educazione alla felicità © RCS Libri SpA 2008
English translation © Howard Curtis 2009

This edition first published in 2009 by
Pushkin Press
12 Chester Terrace
London N1 4ND

British Library Cataloguing in Publication Data:
A catalogue record for this book is available
from the British Library

ISBN 978 1 906548 11 7

Cover: *Kanchanjanga* Gaganendranath Tagore
© National Gallery of Modern Art New Delhi

Inside cover: *Kirche Carona* 1923 Hermann Hesse © Heiner Hesse Arcegno
Häuser am Waldrand 1929 Hermann Hesse © Heiner Hesse Arcegno

Frontispiece: Rabranath Tagore 1916 D M Bennett
Courtesy of the Library of Congress Washington DC

Frontispiece: Hermann Hesse c 1950 Martin Hesse
© Suhrkamp Verlag

Cover flap: Flavia Arzeni 2008
Courtesy of the Author

Set in 10.5 on 13.5 Monotype Baskerville
and printed in the UK by by T J International

FLAVIA ARZENI

AN EDUCATION IN
HAPPINESS

Translated from the Italian
by Howard Curtis

PUSHKIN PRESS
LONDON

INTRODUCTION

A few years ago, I happened to be in Montagnola, a small village near Lugano in the Swiss canton of Ticino, sitting beside the entrance to the museum next door to the house where Hermann Hesse lived for many years, and watching the visitors as they went in to look at photographs, manuscripts and other mementoes of the writer's long, troubled life. It was an average day, in an average year, but I was struck by the number of people there and by the looks of expectation on their faces. Many were young, but there was certainly no shortage of older people, including some who were quite elderly, and they seemed to be from every social class—the kind of people you could see any morning buying a paper from a news-stand or waiting at the bus stop.

What I knew about Hermann Hesse at that time was what someone of my age and profession could not help but know.

I had read most of his work, had attended a conference about him some time earlier, and had assigned graduation theses on him to some of my students. But that day, sitting by the entrance to that small museum, I saw with my own eyes, in the uninterrupted flood of visitors drawn there by nothing more than the desire to get closer to the memory of Hesse, the extraordinary fascination this idiosyncratic writer continues to exert—almost fifty years after his death and almost a hundred after writing his most famous novels—on millions of people who read his books, share his ideas, and flock to the village of Montagnola in large numbers to feel close to him.

Hesse was well aware that his fame, as demonstrated by the thousands of letters he received in the last years of his life, derived not only from the undeniable literary quality of his work, but also from the fact that it deals with the great questions of human existence—where are we, where are we going, what can we do to make a little easier the perennial search for a peaceful life and some form of happiness?

Some years later, in a small town in East Bengal, I observed that a similar kind of popular cult exists in India around the figure of the great Indian poet Rabindranath Tagore. The museum dedicated to his memory in Santiniketan, and his various houses there—as well as his family's home in Calcutta—are also the objects of a constant, silent pilgrimage which reminded me of what I had seen in Montagnola.

Seeing that brought back a memory—of the day I had first set foot in an old house by the sea where I was to live for a considerable length of time. Looking at the spines of the books in the library of the house, I noticed seven or eight volumes of Tagore, elegantly bound, in an Italian edition published around the time of the First World War. I pulled one out at random. It was a collection of poetry, and someone had annotated it in places. Some words, such as 'joy', 'harmony' and 'consolation' had been repeatedly underlined, and I took this as a good omen, as if I were being given clues to the secret of a happy life.

It struck me then that Tagore's vast literary output, like Hesse's, may contain some clues as to how to find a more balanced way of facing the storms of life and to approach that rare, fleeting state of mind to which we give the name 'happiness'.

It was that reflection and that memory that gave me the idea of investigating the lives and works of these two writers, contemporaries of one another, who, starting from quite different places, worked towards the same goal. One moved from West to East, the other from East to West; one led a troubled, contradictory existence, the other was born into a world of comfort and privilege; one was shy and difficult, the other outgoing and eloquent. Yet both had a very similar insight—to attain happiness, one needs only a few things—a close bond with, and acceptance of, nature; a respect for small things and humble tasks; an idea of love that transcends the desire for possession; and finally, an awareness that, to get close to wisdom and truth, it is necessary to go beyond the boundaries of one's own native culture and religion and draw also on the teachings of other religions and other cultures.

Neither Hesse nor Tagore ever expressed these beliefs in a treatise or breviary on happiness. In addition, Hesse experienced, as did many of those close to him, some of the typical ills of our time—anxiety, a sense of solitude, depression, a death wish. Whatever lessons we may derive from him are contained not only in the many seeds strewn throughout his literary work, but also in the painful elements of his life. Whole generations have looked and continue to look to him, as they have to Tagore, as to a mysterious, sometimes enigmatic master with a simple, reassuring message. It is that message that this investigation aims to bring to light.

I have complemented my research by creating a garden on the border between Tuscany and Umbria inspired by those which Hermann Hesse cultivated during his lifetime and tended so passionately; it serves as a place for reflection on the ideas of happiness propounded by these two authors, as presented in this book.

PILGRIMAGES TO
HAPPINESS?

E VERY ONE OF THE MORE than six billion men and women in the world today aspires to be happy. Even a baby, as soon as it comes into the world, before it has either reason or words, desires happiness and, if it can, indicates with a smile when it has achieved it. But if you could ask each of those six billion men and women what happiness is, almost nobody would give you the same answer. In fact, many of them would probably answer that it is impossible to say what happiness is. Does being happy derive from being virtuous, as some ancient Greeks asserted? Or does it lie in a balanced enjoyment of the benefits of the body and the mind, as Aristotle said? Or in detachment from the passions, as it was for the Stoics? Or in being wise? Or in getting closer to God, as any believer—today, as in the past—would tell you? Or in satisfying material needs, as asserted in those doctrines that value the needs of society above those of the individual?

How difficult, if not impossible, it is to find a definition for happiness is demonstrated by the United States Constitution, which includes the pursuit of happiness as one of the inalienable rights of man, but does not define it in concrete terms, leaving this open to interpretation.

As with the idea of beauty, it is easier to speak of the idea of happiness through examples, especially from literature. There are many one could quote, but that would take another book. One of the most beautiful, most famous and most surprising is this passage from a story by Katherine Mansfield: "What can you do if you are thirty and, turning the corner of your own street, you are overcome suddenly by a feeling of bliss—absolute bliss!—as though you'd suddenly swallowed a bright piece of

15

that late afternoon sun and it burned in your bosom, sending out a little shower of sparks into every particle, into every finger and toe? ... "[1]

Hesse, too, in a brief memoir, uses the image of being flooded with a fragment of sun. Having looked for happiness in reading and writing, and having given more pleasure to other people with his work than he had derived from it himself, he had to go back to his years of childhood to find an image of happiness: "One morning I woke up, a lively child of about ten, with a totally strange but delightful feeling of joy and well-being, which like an inner sun went through me with its rays, as if at that moment, in that instant of awakening from a child's sound sleep, something new and wonderful had happened ... I knew nothing of yesterday or tomorrow, but was enveloped and softly lapped by a happy today."[2]

Happiness is not a 'thing', not an objective fact, but an individual, elusive and almost always temporary state born out of the relationship we have with 'something'. It does not necessarily find expression in loving, which can in fact be a cause of unhappiness, but in a certain relationship we have with the loved person. It does not come from the body, but from the relationship we have with our bodies. Its character, in other words, is intimately bound up with each person's subjective nature.

It is hardly surprising, therefore, that with the development of studies on man this theme has gone beyond the confines of philosophy and religion and has increasingly become the subject of scientific research, in fields ranging from psychology to biology, and from sociology to the neurosciences. The shelves of bookshops are full of popular books on happiness and how it can be achieved. Not a day goes by without a conference or festival being held, or a book or film produced, with happiness as its theme. All these are signs of a growing belief that happiness is not due solely to external circumstances, to our genetic makeup, to health or wealth, but is the result of a state of mind; that, to attain it, it is not enough to try to change the things around us—we have to change ourselves. This presupposes, of course, that we have the ability to have an effect on our minds and control our thoughts, and that we are not dealing with actual pathologies, mental disorders or forms of severe depression, to which we can respond only with medicine, drugs, or appropriate forms of psychotherapy. It is a question, first and foremost, of being able to cope with an emotional reality that is common to the vast majority of men and women—the fact that we experience negative feelings and unpleasant events more intensely than positive or pleasant ones. If the media usually present more bad news than good, and give more prominence to acts of violence than acts of kindness, it is not just because people love scandal. It is simply because evil makes a greater impression on our imagination and sensibility than does good.

Even historically, the nature of happiness has been less studied and less commented on than its opposite, the nature of unhappiness and pain, precisely because of an awareness that the negative elements of existence occupy an overriding place in men's thoughts. In fact, the whole Romantic movement, which has had so much influence on European cultural life over the past two centuries, focused on the darker elements of life and the anxious, troubled aspects of the personality.

It is no coincidence that today we know more about the negative dimension, the dark side of our psyches, than we do about the more positive aspects—depressive states, anxieties, fears and phobias have been studied in much greater depth than the mechanisms that produce conditions of well-being. Nor is it a coincidence that literature more frequently deals with sorrow, anxiety and torment than joy and happiness. Happiness is in fact often perceived as a non-event, something that cannot be described or does not deserve to be described. As Tolstoy puts it so well in the first lines of *Anna Karenina*: "All happy families

17

resemble one another, every unhappy family is unhappy in its own way."[3] Or André Gide, when he wonders in *The Immoralist*: "What would there be in a story of happiness?"

There are, in fact, few modern poets or novelists who are remembered not only for the intrinsic quality of their work, but also for the positive teachings present in it—the conception of life it conveys, the crutches it provides a limping, suffering mankind. One of these few is, of course, Tolstoy who, even though he wrote about tragic events, unhappy lives and wars, did represent, for certain people at one time, a new model of open-mindedness, tolerance, pacifism and desire for simplicity. Something similar may be said of Goethe, who has been considered by many generations as not only the greatest German poet, but also a teacher of the art of living and a symbol of the balance and wisdom we associate with the idea of happiness. These were rare, isolated figures, who enlightened the centuries in which they lived. And yet, even in their cases, their reputations with succeeding generations owe more to their artistic and literary message than whatever message of reassurance and comfort they may have wanted to convey.

This is not the case, however, with our two authors, equally popular, but in very different parts of the world—Hermann Hesse and Rabindranath Tagore.

Both men lived through years of crisis, war, unrest and social upheaval at the end of the nineteenth century and in the first decades of the twentieth century, but belonged to profoundly different cultures—one to the vast culture of Europe, the other to the great civilisation of India. They sought happiness in similar ways—not by dominating nature but by being in tune with it; not by desiring to possess what is large but by growing closer to what is small; not with great feats but with patient practice and constant work; not through the mechanical observance of a religion or a tradition but by trying to find the truth in different cultures. The value of their work does not derive only from its artistic quality, but also from the advice it contains for living more happily, drawing on a cultural and literary heritage that unites West and East, and bringing the conduct of the individual back into harmony with the world that surrounds him. That is why they have found great fame both during their lifetimes and since.

And that is why, every year, thousands of visitors descend on a small museum in the village of Montagnola, in the hills overlooking Lake Lugano, to follow in the footsteps of Hesse. On another lake, Constance, there is an even smaller village, Gaienhofen, where the writer lived for only a few years in the first decade of the twentieth century. Here, too, enthusiasts come to visit his house and tread the paths where he used to walk.

A mirror image of the cult exists in a very different part of the world—north-east India—in the remote village where Rabindranath Tagore founded first an experimental school and then his international university Visva-Bharati, and in Calcutta, where the former Tagore family residence has also become a museum and is the goal of a constant pilgrimage by Indians and non-Indians alike.

These are not just examples of cultural tourism. By visiting Hesse's and Tagore's homes and following their daily routines the crowds are searching for their message, their answers to the question: 'How do we become—and how do we stay—happy?'

The theme of harmony and serenity runs through the fiction, poetry and essays of both men, and even more through their reflections, letters and autobiographical writings. At a distance of almost a century from when they were written, their works are still read all over the world, and are reissued in the form of anthologies or thematic collections, as is done with the thoughts of the great masters. And this is what they were—masters of the rare art of helping others to live, helping the young to overcome the storms of youth and the old to live with the paralysing stillness of old age.

Hesse and Tagore were not consistently famous, and there were times when their reputations suffered a decline. At periods during their lifetimes, and after their deaths, reservations about their work were expressed by academic critics. This is hardly surprising—for the reasons already stated, it is impossible to judge these authors merely in terms of literary quality, separate from the human message that permeates their art.

Hesse found success immediately with his first novel, *Peter Camenzind*, a success repeated with a strange, cryptic work, *Demian*, which was particularly appreciated by the young, and then again, ten years later, with a book that has remained consistently popular, *Narziss and Goldmund*. But his official consecration came in 1946, when he was awarded the Nobel Prize—an award which was not unconnected with Hesse's dissident stand, first against militarism, then against Nazism. In the immediate aftermath of the Second World War, however, there were those who, in a Germany where it seemed impossible to separate literature from politics, distanced themselves from an author they considered an apostle of the inner life and the prophet of an outdated individualism. But his fame grew again to extraordinary heights in the 1960s and 1970s, first in America and then throughout the world, thanks to two books in particular; two books that can still be considered central to his output—*Siddhartha* and *Steppenwolf.*

In the course of a generally retiring, inward-looking existence, Hesse was not unaware of the extraordinary stir his books and ideas caused in the outside world. This had nothing to do with vanity or ambition. His success demonstrated to him that his metaphors and teachings had struck a genuine chord and indicated how the seeds he had sown might flower in the future. So many admirers wanted to see him in person, especially in his final years, that, to protect himself, he had to put a sign on the gate of his house telling visitors to "walk by, as if nobody lived here". But when it came to writing, he was both generous with his time and conscientious—although he obviously could not answer all the tens of thousands of letters he was sent in his life the many letters from him that have survived demonstrate how concerned he was to advise and reassure his correspondents.

Tagore, too, was a cult figure and has remained so in India, whereas in the West the huge popularity he enjoyed in the first decades of the last century faded during the more political period that art went through after the Second World War. Like Hesse, he was a precocious writer, translated into several languages when he was still young, but it was above all his volume of poems called *Gitanjali* that spread his fame in the West and gained him the enthusiastic admiration of two giants of literature—Ezra Pound and W B Yeats—as demonstrated by Yeats's beautiful introduction to his first collection translated into English. Nor did he lack for official recognition—from the knighthood conferred on him by the British government to the most sought-after honour of all, the Nobel Prize for Literature, which he was awarded in 1913. However, his relations with the British soon deteriorated. These were the years when the first tears began to appear in the fabric of the vast British Empire and London adopted an intransigent policy towards the movement for Indian independence. In 1919, after the violent repression in the Punjab known as the Amritsar Massacre, an indignant Tagore returned his knighthood. This did nothing to diminish his fame, in fact it may even have increased it, and it grew even further when he began travelling tirelessly. Wherever he went— from France to Sweden; from Argentina to the United States he was greeted as a celebrity. In Germany he found a remarkable mentor in Count Hermann Keyserling, himself a distinguished man of letters with a deep knowledge of India, who went with him from city to city, lecture to lecture, and introduced him to a public that responded with an enthusiasm sometimes verging on hysteria. In the years immediately following the First World War, Germany was going through a dramatic period of crisis and uncertainty. Humiliated by their defeat and the conditions of the peace imposed by the victors, their economy shattered, their currency worthless, surrounded by a hostile Europe, many Germans were attracted to Tagore's clear, noble, accessible poetic language, and his unusual, austere persona. Among his admirers, he numbered poets and writers such as Rainer Maria Rilke and Stefan Zweig.

Hesse never met Tagore. He knew his work and even wrote reviews of *Gitanjali*, *The Gardener* and *The Home and the World*. When it came to Tagore's personality, however, and the effect he had on public opinion, Hesse always maintained a certain reserve. Perhaps he was disconcerted by this very 'European' Easterner, this poet with such a liking for applause. Or perhaps he sensed in Tagore's prophetic message a desire to be a guide for posterity that was not dissimilar from his own. They may have respected one another intellectually, but—despite so many affinities—they kept their distance. And yet Hesse and Tagore are in a way complementary. What unites them above all is that for both men, their conception of life and their vision of the world were just as important as their poetic and literary work. While it may have been the latter that brought them into the limelight, it was the former that ensured that their names were surrounded with an aura of myth and legend. Coming from different worlds and different cultural spheres, Hesse and Tagore both moved towards ideals of harmony, happiness and wisdom which went beyond the merely contingent. As writers, both men were consistent and obsessive, tackling the same themes over and over—the primary role of nature in human existence, the importance of work and of love for one's fellow men, the joy of small everyday things, the essential function of art, and the reconciling of different cultures and religions within a single great unity that transcends space and time.

A DISCIPLINED REBEL

A STRANGE TEACHER

T O JUDGE FROM HIS LIFE, Hesse would seem an unlikely teacher of happiness. He had a disturbed adolescence marked by rebellion against his teachers and parents, and a young manhood full of doubts and anxieties, which resulted in a constant desire for movement, especially on foot. He was a bundle of contradictions, frequently in crisis, torn between asceticism and sensuality, between an aspiration towards peace and quiet and a hunger for knowledge, between a desire for order and a wish to break up the family.

How is it possible, we may wonder, that this man—subject to depressions and to chronic psychosomatic and physical ailments, afflicted by pains in his eyes and joints, tortured by migraine and sleepless nights, and so devoured by anxiety that he several times contemplated suicide—how is it possible that this man managed not only to survive, but to find, at a certain point in his life, a kind of harmony and balance that allowed him to reach his eighty-fifth birthday unscathed? And how is it possible that this bundle of misery has become a cult figure for millions of readers, for many generations, as confused today as they were in the past, who find in his writings answers to the questions that plague their lives?

Calw is a small town in the Black Forest, in the German state of Baden-Württemberg, surrounded by woods and gentle hills. It was here that Hermann Hesse was born in 1877, and here that he spent the first years of his life. In fact, he was to spend almost the whole of his life in remote localities in the southern part of Germany or in Switzerland, with only brief periods in cities such as Basle, Bern or Zurich. The tranquil landscapes of his childhood left such an indelible mark on him and on his work that during his old age he would continue to draw on the same world of images, which was always an anchor and a refuge for him in the storms of life.

At the time Calw was the centre of an active Pietist community. Pietism was a religious movement within German Protestantism which placed the individual's search for God above the dogmatism of the organised Church, although Hesse's family also belonged to the latter. Both his father and his maternal grandfather were missionaries, and his mother, a central figure in the writer's life, made sure that his education was based on unshakable moral principles and a clear distinction between what is lawful and what is forbidden; between what faith teaches us and what leads us to sin. But alongside this strict provincial ethos, there was another aspect to Hesse's family, no less important for the development of his vision of the world; an aspect that encouraged a more open, tolerant and cosmopolitan outlook. It was his maternal grandfather, Hermann Gundert, who knew various European and oriental languages, had studied Sanskrit and had spent many years in India, who left the deepest mark on his personality. Hesse thus had a cultural background that combined two opposing visions—one dogmatic, the other inquisitive and unorthodox. Over time this contrast came to be not only a source of anxiety to him but also one of intellectual and spiritual richness.

So it was that Hesse became familiar from an early age with two religious strands—Christianity in the form of a strict Pietism and Indian spirituality. The Hesse household, as he himself recalled, was one in which different worlds met—where the Holy Scriptures were read and Eastern philosophy was discussed: "Many worlds came together in that house. We read the Bible and prayed, we studied Indian philosophy and applied it, we played excellent music, we learned about Buddha and Lao-Tzu, and many guests arrived from different countries."[4]

AGAINST ALL RULES

HESSE WAS FOUR when his family moved to Basle and nine when he returned to Calw, where he began attending a 'Latin school' in preparation for being admitted to a famous evangelical theological seminary at the monastery of Maulbronn. But his school years were an ordeal—he hated and feared his teachers, and was a reluctant, inattentive student. At fourteen he did in fact begin studying at the Maulbronn seminary, but only six months later he ran away, with no money in his pockets and no coat on his back, to face the rigours of winter. He was found and brought back, but was soon expelled. The following years were marked by constant crisis—unwilling to accept any kind of teaching, he was rejected by school after school. All his family's efforts to give him an education in keeping with the principles of the household failed, and he spent time in a mental home and a correctional institution. His scandalous behaviour culminated in a suicide attempt. At this point, Hermann broke off relations with his family, abandoned his studies and began work, first as an apprentice in a clock factory, and then, at the age of eighteen, as an apprentice bookseller in Tübingen. He had already decided some years earlier to, as he put it, "become a poet, or nothing at all", and had begun a process of personal cultural education, independent of all academic rules, acquiring the habit, which would remain with him throughout his life, of reading avidly in his free time.

The rigid, authoritarian educational system of his time would leave its mark on Hesse, as would the feelings of restlessness and rebellion which that system provoked. There are traces of this in a novel with the significant title *Beneath the Wheel*, in which the main character is endlessly forced to compete at school, and his lack of freedom eventually drives him to suicide.

These were the founding years of the Empire, when the Germans were busy constructing a strong Germany, imbued with positivistic philosophy and nationalistic in spirit. With the ascent to the throne of Wilhelm II, the industrial infrastructure expanded, and an extraordinary amount of technical and scientific development catapulted Germany into the top rank of world powers. As in every period of transformation, this new-found wealth was accompanied by social unrest and class conflict.

The whole of Hesse's life and work can be read in two ways— on the one hand as a reaction to an individual crisis, and on the other as a response to the social crisis of his time.

Many of Hesse's characteristic themes—the unnatural effects of the great changes then taking place in Germany, the frenetic pace of industrialisation and urbanisation, the weight of a rigidly hierarchical social structure, and on the other hand the refusal to submit to the principle of duty for duty's sake or efficiency at all costs and the rejection of the widespread cult of nationalism—are specific products of the environment and the time in which Hesse was born and grew up.

He was still in his early twenties when he started to publish his first poems and literary reviews, the latter an activity he would pursue for the rest of his life. He was, in fact, to become a tireless critic with wide-ranging interests, from literature to philosophy, religion to art. Hesse never belonged to any literary coterie or intellectual movement, and never hid his indifference to such labels: "What do I care if such and such a writer is a symbolist, a naturalist, a pupil of Maeterlinck or a friend of [Stefan] George?" he wrote when he was not yet thirty. "I want to know if he has something worthwhile to tell me, if his book could be a friend, a comforter, or merely a way of passing time."[5]

THE APPRENTICE WANDERER

I N 1901 HESSE MADE HIS FIRST JOURNEY TO ITALY, travelling by train—in third-class carriages—or on foot, spending a long time in Venice and Florence and also visiting the beautiful cities of the Italian provinces, from Padua to Ravenna, from Arezzo to Assisi. He also liked small towns off the beaten track in Umbria and Tuscany, where he would spend the evenings in taverns, with the customary glass of Chianti in his hand. He had been a passionate reader of books on the Italian Renaissance and, whether he was looking at a Giotto, a Raphael Madonna or a Perugino, almost always demonstrated critical acumen, a marked sensitivity to colour and an independence of judgement. The figure that attracted him the most was that of the great saint, Saint Francis, about whom he wrote a biography *Francis of Assisi*, a work which clearly demonstrates Hesse's sense of personal involvement. What he saw in Saint Francis was not only the man of religion, a figure at once mystical and profoundly close to the beauty of creation, but also some kind of kindred spirit; someone who had set out to find a way of life through which he could be in harmony with himself, the world and God.

Hesse often asked himself, in those early years of the twentieth century, what restlessness drove him to his travels, why he returned to places he already knew, and why he went so often to Italy. Was it a desire for escape, was it because of his love of art, or was it something else entirely?

Hesse's answers were always existential and revolved around the great questions of the meaning and purpose of human life. When Hesse admired the works of the old masters, or the architecture of a cathedral or a nobleman's palace, what he saw in them was an unexpected consolation for the agonising solitude in which human beings spend their lives.

But there was another, more down-to-earth element in his passion for Italy. Hesse was attracted by the South, by the sun and the light, and it was no coincidence that, when he was over forty, he would settle in the canton of Ticino, the southernmost area among those close to the regions of his childhood, where he would remain until his death. Hesse seems in a way to have realised intuitively what we now take for granted in the diagnosis and cure of many depressive syndromes—the beneficial, invigorating and restorative effects of sun and light.

By the time he undertook his second Italian journey, Hesse was no longer alone. He went with a group of friends, among them Maria Bernoulli, a sensitive, difficult woman, whom he would marry the year after the journey. Maria, or Mia as she was called, was nine years older than he was, and Hesse may have been seeking a mother figure. His own mother, whom he had so loved and feared, had died the previous year. With Mia, Hesse settled in a peasant house in Gaienhofen hoping to find in a stable relationship with a woman and in a simple rural existence the peace of mind that had so far eluded him. This new life seemed to bring him luck—in 1904, his novel *Peter Camenzind* was published and was highly praised. Inspired by the canons and ideals of Romanticism, the book is a hymn of praise to the redeeming force of nature, seen as pure, uncontaminated beauty, in contrast to a degraded and corrupt urban world. As a result of his sudden fame, Hesse was invited to contribute to a number of magazines. His second book, the above-mentioned *Beneath the Wheel*, was a similar success.

Hesse would seem to have had every reason to be happy. He was becoming a well-known writer, had a wife with whom he shared many interests, especially a passion for music and nature, in 1905 his first son, Bruno, was born, and a year later he was able to build his own large house just outside the village. He was surrounded by a congenial group of friends—painters, musicians and writers—and could claim to have become the kind of respected intellectual he had aspired to be since he was a young boy. And yet he did not feel at ease—his new-found security aroused his suspicions and his well-ordered life filled him with a sense of unease. Here he is, on a tranquil evening on Lake Constance, sitting at his desk, reading a book by candlelight, his wife at the piano, the countryside silent around them. But, instead of peace, he can feel that old restlessness that has tormented him since his youth welling up within him. And the question comes into his mind: "Are you really happy?"[6]

Hesse could not, in fact, hide his own contradictions from himself, torn as he was between the need for security and its rejection; between the desire for freedom demanded by his artistic vocation and the family ties with which he had bound himself. These inner psychological conflicts had their corollary in a large number of psychosomatic illnesses which plagued him to such an extent that he was driven to seek help in a nursing home.

His old restlessness returned, and a vague sense of Sehnsucht, a sense of wistful longing, led him increasingly to abandon his home and travel, or simply wander, leaving his wife to take care of their sons alone—his second son Heiner having been born in 1909, and his third son, Martin, in 1911.

It was in that year that Hesse took the only long journey of his life, when he and a painter friend set off for the East Indies from Genoa on board a comfortable steam ship. The journey lasted several months and took him to Sumatra, in the Dutch East Indies, Singapore and Ceylon, but not to the Indian subcontinent, even though it was there that his desires and thoughts were mostly directed.

The idea of escaping an outworn Western civilisation in search of the East and rediscovering oneself was fashionable at the time among European intellectuals, as evidenced by the great novels of Joseph Conrad published in those years, such as *Lord Jim* and *The Nigger of the Narcissus*. For Hesse, the East also represented a search for the land of his mother's birth

31

and that magical, mysterious world whose air he had breathed since he was a child. But his travel diaries and notes, which were published in 1913 under the geographically misleading title *From India*, testify to the fact that this experience, in which he had placed great hopes, fell short of his imagination.

Hesse came back from the journey earlier than planned, fascinated by the virgin forest and the luxuriant vegetation but vexed by the tropical heat and the food, and worried about their possible effects on his health. The native peoples he had encountered, especially the Indians and the Malays, had seemed to him very different from the paragons of natural nobility he had imagined, and his notes betray a certain admiration and esteem only for the Chinese. The presence in the East of a spiritual dimension that Europe had lost did not escape him, but he was not yet ready to make it his and assimilate it fully. The journey, in any case, had not relieved his anxieties—it would be some time before Hesse realised that it was not enough to travel a long way from home to find sources of wisdom, and that replacing Europe with the East did not represent an answer. The emptiness he felt inside himself would only be filled when he was able to combine the spirituality of the latter and the cultural traditions of the former.

On his return however, Hesse realised that the experience of leading a basically isolated life, in close contact with a woman from whom he had gradually become estranged—their marriage now irreparably in crisis—was doomed to failure. It occurred to him that living closer to a city might be a viable alternative, and he decided to move with his family to an old villa just outside Bern in Switzerland, surrounded by a delightful garden full of flowers, bushes and tall old trees. But not even the pleasantness of this environment would succeed in curing his ills.

WAR AND PEACE

IN 1914, Hesse's personal problems were eclipsed by his awareness of the impending tragedy looming over Europe. He had
now been living in Switzerland for two years and viewed the outbreak of war—which was initially greeted with enthusiasm by
much of the German intelligentsia—as a devastating, traumatic
event. At first he hesitated, torn between his moral convictions
and his feelings of solidarity with his country. He even volun-
teered for the army, but was rejected. He then took an explicitly
pacifist stand, and, in an article that appeared that same year in
the Swiss newspaper the *Neue Zürcher Zeitung,* he appealed to the
nations of Europe to remember that the values of the classical
world and of humanism, as well as those of the Christian tradition, constituted the most precious heritage of their civilisation.
It was the duty of intellectuals to encourage dialogue between
nations, to build bridges between peoples, to oppose hate and
death with life.

Hesse became involved in a centre set up in Bern to supply
books and aid to German prisoners of war in France, and to
those who had been interned in Switzerland, but his stand was
not greatly appreciated in Germany and helped to make him
an isolated figure within German cultural circles, where he
was looked on with suspicion. The whole of Europe was being
swept by a wave of nationalism, and there were few writers
mobilising for peace rather than war. Among these few were
Stefan Zweig, Yvan Goll and Romain Rolland, with whom
Hesse established relations and was to remain friendly for many
years to come. It seems paradoxical that a writer like Hesse,
so often accused of having been remote from politics and of

having shown indifference towards the great challenges of his time, should in fact have been one of those who was most clear-sighted about the dangers of those authoritarian, nationalistic and racist tendencies of German society which brought Hitler to power, even going so far as to renounce his citizenship and become a Swiss national as early as 1923. "This Hitler, whom you consider to have only become power-hungry and dangerous in 1933, was already perfectly recognisable in 1923 to anyone who had their eyes open," he would write in a letter to Thomas Mann.[7]

The war years were especially painful for Hesse. The scale of the slaughter was all too evident in the news coming from the various fronts, and the writer took it as a sign of the disintegration of the culture and values of Old Europe which, in a way, were also his. On a personal level, 1916 was a year of disasters. His father died, one of his sons became seriously ill, he was beset with money worries, and his wife, who for some time had been showing signs of serious mental disturbance, had to be admitted to a psychiatric clinic. Feeling under siege from the outside world and fragile in his own inner world, Hesse fell into a state of depression. In order not to go under, he decided to try psychoanalysis, which was becoming popular at the time, and consulted a pupil of Carl Gustav Jung.

THE INVESTIGATION OF THE SELF

U P UNTIL THE FIRST WORLD WAR nature had been an anchor for him—a romantically exalted nature which welcomes men like a great mother and opens up a magical, multi-faceted world. It had often, if not always, been the background, and sometimes even the main character of his works. But the war had instilled in him a new awareness of the fact that man has to search for a cure for his suffering inside, as well as outside, himself. Jungian analysis, he thought, would be a tool with which to achieve this. With his young psychoanalyst, Josef Bernhard Lang, Hesse established a relationship of trust and friendship which would last for a considerable time. It would also leave a deep imprint on his literary work, which, from this point on, would be increasingly filled with symbols and archetypes from Jungian theory, marking out the path that would lead him to examine the 'inner life', the individual consciousness—for the basis of all change, whether moral, political or social.

In psychoanalysis, and the theories of Freud and Jung, Hesse had found a tool with which to investigate and understand his own anxieties—the feeling, which had never left him, of incurable nostalgia for his childhood, the sense of solitude which he invariably projected onto his characters, his restlessness and constant need to be elsewhere, the temptation towards self-destruction and suicide. In a short essay of 1918, *Artists and Psychoanalysis*, he talks about the vast amount of hidden material which analysis brings to the surface, making it possible for an artist to draw on his dreams, associations and memories by putting his conscious mind in contact with his unconscious.

This process of metamorphosis, of 'reawakening' of consciousness, has many echoes in his poetry and fiction. The most significant, perhaps, is in his novel *Demian*, written while he was still in analysis and published under the pen name Sinclair, perhaps to indicate a break with his previous works or perhaps to divert the critics' hasty judgments of an undeniably complex and ambiguous text onto a non-existent author.

Demian traces the inner journey of Emil Sinclair, through the apparently irreconcilable realms of good and evil, light and darkness, order and chaos, instinct and reason, knowledge and ignorance. It is about the growth of awareness, and subsequent overcoming, of the dualism between antithetic elements which coexist within the psyche of each person and which come together in a unity that reflects the polarity of the cosmos.

In one of the most significant passages in the book Hesse writes: "An enlightened man had but one duty—to seek the way to himself, to reach inner certainty, to grope his way forwards, no matter where it led."[8] The revolution in content represented by *Demian* is matched by a revolution in style, language and narrative structure, with its world of obscure symbolic images, oneiric and esoteric elements and references to ancient myths.

Many works by Hesse feature characters in search of themselves, who confront the difficult theme of the relationship between art and life, and it is easy to recognise here a problem that tormented Hesse himself. If he never wrote an autobiography, it was because there was no need—his writings are in fact one vast autobiography, in which the most significant events of his life are reflected. This was the beginning of a new phase in his literary output, the period of 'biographies of the mind', which each centre on a single character's inner journey from one life to another, from one state to another. Such works may take different literary forms, sometimes travel diaries, or rather 'pilgrimage' diaries, sometimes novels that trace the development of a character's mind and spirit.

Within an enquiry which tended increasingly to the analysis of the being and the mutations of the ego, there was a broadening of subject matter—the already-noted themes of adolescent crisis, rebellion against the middle-class world, growing industrialisation, the conflict between the world of the great cities and the country, wandering and the decline of European civilisation are joined by others, the result of new experiences and new readings within the realm of Indian and Chinese philosophy and religion, all of which would be interwoven repeatedly in his literary work.

As for the rule he had given himself to seek out his own path, wherever it might lead, Hesse applied it strictly. He left the family home for good and went to live by himself in Casa Camuzzi, a strange building resembling a baroque hunting castle, in the small village of Montagnola, surrounded by hills of vineyards and chestnut woods, in the canton of Ticino. Here he would spend some of the most intense and creative years of his life.

When the war was over, Hesse did not forget his commitment to a moral renewal of German society, and in his writings he addressed the young people of his country, exhorting them to leave the past behind them and seek out a new, independent vision of society.

He himself had turned his back on the past. The summer of 1919, when he arrived in Ticino, was exceptionally bright and warm, and it unleashed a new burst of energy in Hesse which found expression in an explosion of creativity, including a famous story called *Klingsor's Last Summer*, which tells of a painter's last days of madness and intoxication.

Stimulated by the landscapes and colours of Ticino, he spent a great deal of time painting, especially watercolours, working in the open air, in physical contact with nature. He had begun painting some years earlier, partly out of his own inclination, and partly at the prompting of his psychoanalyst. Now he found in it a way to express himself in the most joyful manner possible, as well as, unexpectedly, a means to achieve balance and pleasure. His watercolours are a triumph of light and colour—reds, yellows, deep blues—and the same subjects recur constantly—the landscape around him, the fields, the hills, the mountains, the lake, a few solitary houses or churches. Like his novels and stories, his watercolours are the visible expression of a long search, and constitute a liberating, therapeutic tool and an unexpected source of happiness.

Hesse had a changeable temperament, and his state of mind never stayed the same for long. This period of euphoria at his regained freedom and creativity was succeeded by moments of unproductiveness and anxiety, which again led him to seek psychoanalytical help. This time he turned directly to the master, Carl Gustav Jung, in person. Solitude, which had been a cause of joy, had become a burden. In addition, there were new financial difficulties. He sought and found comfort in the help of a few Swiss acquaintances, in friendships with a number of painters, and in a close bond with the writer Hugo Ball, who would later write his biography.

Meanwhile, Hesse, despite periods of uncertainty and long interruptions, continued working on one of his major novels, *Siddhartha*, which appeared in 1922. The book again charts a spiritual journey. This time it is the journey of Siddhartha, the son of a Brahman, who leaves his family home to search for the true path. At first, he decides to imitate the sages and ascetics, and embarks on a regime of fasting and meditation. He soon realises, however, that no doctrine, however noble and elevated, can give him what he is looking for—something to which he cannot yet give a name. He therefore decides to abandon the spiritual path and to immerse himself in the world of the senses, enjoying to the full what the 'childlike people' desire the most— wealth, success, the pleasures of the flesh. Before long, though, he wearies of this world of appearances, too, and distances himself from it. The thing that makes it possible for him to rise again is his meeting with the ferryman Vasudeva, from whom he learns the mysteries of the river. The flow of time is associated with the flow of the waters, and in their flow all things and all changes become unity, everything is interwoven and finds its justification. The world is like the river, where good and evil, pleasure and pain meet and everything flows, and the voice of the river is the voice of life.

Siddhartha, too, is a fragment of Hesse's biography; a fragment with a happy ending, as it were, in which, in the guise of an Indian fable, an individual seeks, and finds, the harmony of the world. It is a product of the familiarity he had gradually acquired with Indian and Chinese philosophy; the expression of an all-encompassing vision, where the rejection of dogma and the idea of a unity in which all religions merge is reconciled with the lessons of Christianity.

WAVERING

B UT JUST AS EVERYTHING FLOWS, so everything is repeated.
Hesse's journey towards serenity, balance and a certain
kind of happiness would seem to have been over by this point,
inner peace finally attained. But more years of trial and error
awaited him.

In 1923, his rheumatic pains drove him to visit the spa town
of Baden, near Zurich, and this would become a habit he kept
up until almost the end of his life. That visit, and the subsequent
ones, inspired many important passages in his works, many
diary entries, poems and reflections. During his first visit, he
wrote an extremely odd work, its singularity beginning with
the title—*Psychologia Balnearia, or Observations of a Patient at Baden*,
which would be published two years later, in 1925, under the
title *A Guest at the Spa*.

A Guest at the Spa gives us a clue to the philosophy of life towards
which Hesse was slowly moving. In among the descriptions of the
thermal springs, the patients' ailments and their daily routines,
the author shows us the complex psychology of a sick man—
himself—whom he regards with irony and whose condition
he presents as being that of an individual in conflict with his
immediate surroundings and with the world in general:

> *I would like to write whole chapters and sentences in which the melody
> and the countermelody appear simultaneously, in which the manifold
> combines with the homogeneous, the facetious with the serious. To me, in
> fact, life consists of nothing but a wavering between two poles; a coming
> and going between the two fundamental pillars of the world.*[9]

40

Wavering thus from pole to pole, Hesse, now permanently separated from his first wife, met and then married a young singer named Ruth Wenger. This marriage soon proved to be a mistake—Hesse was already having second thoughts by the time of the wedding—and was to end, three years later, in divorce. In Germany, meanwhile, the economic crisis and the dramatic inflation of 1923 wiped out his income, including his royalties. Hesse had to look for new sources of revenue, and he embarked on a series of lectures and public readings of his works, which once again brought him into contact with German literary circles. However the experience was not a very happy one.

Amid these waverings in Hesse's spirit, the winter months spent in Zurich, starting in 1925, formed a singular period—not lacking in distractions—in which he mixed with a group of musicians and painters. For Hesse, who loved the sun and the light, winter was usually a particularly difficult time. These Zurich winters were an exception—he took lessons in modern dance, became interested in the cinema and jazz, visited nightclubs, drank, and flirted with women.

As we might imagine, these were transitory phases, and further inner upheavals awaited him. In the introductory pages of *Crisis*, his verse diary of that time, he describes this chaotic period of his life during which his moral conscience itself seemed to waver and a dark world of instincts and sensuality, previously held in check, rose to the surface. All this forms part of the subject matter of one of the most controversial and disturbing of all his books—*Steppenwolf*. Like Hesse when he wrote it, the protagonist Harry Haller—the identification of character with author is underlined by their shared initials—is approaching his fiftieth birthday. We find again in *Steppenwolf* the sickness of the times, a sense of historical and cultural decadence, an awareness of the fragility of German democracy and a clear-headed vision of new wars and disasters to come.

But this time, facing the threat of complete disintegration, Harry Haller/Hermann Hesse chooses not to escape but to experience to the full his own contradictions and those of the era in which he lives—modern art in the despised forms of mass escapism, the supremacy of technology over the spirit, a society sapped by the irrational and whose freedom is under threat. It is when we touch bottom that we find the spirit to pick ourselves up and start again. Harry Haller toys with the idea of suicide and chooses his fiftieth birthday as the perfect date on which to kill himself; this decision gives him a feeling of regained freedom and strength, which enables him to live in the meantime. In this way, thanks to the constant reminder of death, the *Steppenwolf* succeeds in transforming the temptation of nothingness into "a philosophy favourable to life".[10]

This is the most dramatic and anguished of Hesse's works, and yet it contains the seeds of another, more serene, outlook on life. A sense of humour, an ability to laugh, is, in *Steppenwolf*, the supreme weapon of those who, having confronted the chaos of their own psyches and the world, manage to acquire lightness, to accept even the banality of life and see the demands of their egos in perspective.

Ever since he was a young man, Hesse had fought his own crises and ailments with intense activity, both physical and intellectual—action was always one of his weapons of defence. No sooner had Hesse finished *Steppenwolf* than he began work on a new novel, *Narziss and Goldmund*, which was published in 1930. This level of activity reflected a new stabilising element in his personal life, his relationship with Ninon Dolbin Ausländer, an art historian of Jewish descent, born in Czernowitz on the edges of the Hapsburg Empire, with whom he had been corresponding for some time. From 1927 and for the rest of his life, Ninon would be his stable, intelligent and understanding companion.

In 1931 they married and went to live in large house just outside Montagnola, which a generous Swiss friend had placed at their disposal. It had a splendid view of Lake Lugano and was surrounded by a plot of land, which Hesse transformed into a garden he would love passionately. A new chapter in his life was beginning.

PROSPECTS OF TRANQUILLITY

HIS EXTENSIVE READING about the religions and cultures of East and West was taking root. He no longer felt the compulsive urge to travel—and in fact would travel very little during the rest of his life. He found, in so far as his contradictory, anxious spirit allowed it, a certain balance and something approaching happiness. After the squalls of his youth and the long fogs of his middle years, a balmy autumn ripened the fruits of his mind, which he generously shared with those close to him.

Despite living such a secluded life, Hesse did not isolate himself from the world—he contributed to a number of publishing projects, continued his activities as a critic and essayist, and wrote for newspapers and magazines for as long as it remained possible. But the climate in Germany had become difficult for anyone swimming against the tide. His German publisher, Gottfried Bermann Fischer, was forced to emigrate; Hesse signed a letter of solidarity in his favour. Various magazines refused to publish his contributions, and in 1939 some of his works were banned.

Hesse had seen all this coming for some time. With the advent of Nazism, his home in Switzerland became a transit point for German intellectuals fleeing Germany. Among them were Thomas Mann, with whom he would remain close friends for the rest of his life, Martin Buber, the great writer and scholar of Hebraism, and, later, the writer and painter Peter Weiss, who would stay for a long time in Hesse's house, as well as an uninterrupted succession of other names—some famous, some less so.

Hesse lived history but also learnt how to protect himself from it. He had been fervent in his anti-militaristic crusade during the First World War and now he took up an even more extreme position: "I am against all attempts to change the world by force and so I do not support them, even if they are Socialist, even if they appear obviously just or desirable."[11]

Consistent with his aversion to systems and ideologies, he did not align himself with a party or a political faction, but chose the path of individual, moral and humanitarian commitment. He continued to reply to those who wrote to him in search of help or advice—a habit he maintained, exhausting as it was, into old age.

In the 1930s, while Germany, Italy, Spain and the Soviet Union were creating and consolidating their totalitarian systems, Hesse constructed what may be his most difficult work—*The Glass Bead Game*. In it he conceived the most abstract and sophisticated ideal structure possible, the most complex and improbable system of social organisation and—as we would say today—governance ever imagined. In a period when civilisation is in decline, a group of men set up a worldwide order with the aim of preserving and handing down to those who will come after them the great cultural and spiritual values that mankind has gathered over the centuries. The spiritual rule governing this order is centred on the glass bead game, a mysterious language for initiates which encompasses all that has been created in the sciences and the arts and which the players have to use according to strict rules. The purpose of the game is to find new combinations and connections between all the different areas of knowledge and, at the same time, to dictate the rules of life for the current generations. The world of the Castalia is a utopia where the cult of harmony, the practice of meditation, and the love of truth are achieved through discipline and study, especially the study of music and mathematics.

The highest level that can be reached in the 'game' is lightness, serenity: "To achieve this cheerful serenity is to me, and to many others, the finest and highest goal … Such cheerfulness is neither frivolity nor complacency; it is supreme insight and love … it is indestructible and only increases with age and nearness to death " [12]

Perhaps it was to this lightness that Hesse had always aspired; now, at last, in the final stages of a troubled life, he was getting there, like a road that reaches the summit only after having taken endless twists and turns. In the following pages we shall try to see in concrete terms what lessons can be drawn from that journey.

The Glass Bead Game appeared in Switzerland in 1943 and in Germany three years later. The years immediately after the Second World War saw Hesse laden with awards and honours, the most important, of course, being the Nobel Prize. To celebrate his seventy-fifth birthday, the German publisher Suhrkamp brought out a complete edition of his works.

At this point he was a writer who could take his place, artistically and socially, as one of the greatest of his time. Fame, however, did not change his habits. He continued leading the same retiring, secluded life to which he was accustomed, divided between reading his many books and tending his garden, writing an essay or a poem and listening to a sonata by Mozart. He died on 9th August 1962, in his peaceful house in Montagnola, not far away from the building that now houses the museum that has become the goal of so many fervent pilgrimages. On the evening before his death, he was still working on a version of his last poem, prophetically entitled *The Creak of a Broken Branch*.

HAPPINESS WITHOUT TIME

A ND SO—with a poetic fragment that once again refers to
nature—ended a long life full of questions and dark areas,
often touched by pain and the temptation of death—not only
in Hesse's own thoughts but also, by a strange twist of fate, in
the choices of the people close to him. In 1935 his brother Hans
committed suicide, leaving Hesse with an undefined sense of
guilt, and his first wife, Maria Bernoulli, was repeatedly admitted
to psychiatric hospitals during her life. Even after Hesse's death,
the family tragedy continued—his third son, Martin, would also
take his own life. We must therefore ask ourselves again our original question—what guiding thread led Hesse through his inner
struggles and storms and made it possible for him at last to cast
the anchor of his ship in calm waters?

It was, I believe, the patient search for an idea of happiness
different from the one that consumer society, today as then,
encourages and propagates, linked to wealth, success, physical
appearance, sex and love.

Everywhere in his novels and essays, and in his letters and
notes, we find brief reflections or sudden flashes of illumination
on this subject. Some of them were gathered together in an
essay written in 1949, when Hesse was over seventy, and in fact
called *Happiness*. The point of departure is the question of what
people mean by happiness. And the answer is twofold—at an
individual level happiness means well-being, health, and good
family relations; at a social level it means living in times of
peace and freedom. But experience tells Hesse that both these
things can be deceptive and impermanent. He was born during
a happy time, when Germany was moving into a period of

political stability, prosperity and peace, and he spent his early childhood in a respectable family, all his material needs taken care of. Then his youth turned sour, his reading stoked doubts and uncertainties, his life went through a series of crises and his country was plunged into a war, which ended in a disastrous defeat. Hesse realised that happiness is not ensured by external circumstances, which are uncertain and changeable, and that, if it even exists, it cannot be other than the result of a frame of mind.

As the years passed, Hesse broadened the horizons of his reading, embracing not only Western thought and literature, but also the philosophical and religious heritage of India and, above all, the masters of Chinese wisdom, from Lao-Tzu to Chuang-Tzu, and finally succeeded in formulating his idea of happiness which he expressed in this way: "By happiness today I mean something totally objective, in other words totality itself, being without time, the eternal music of the world, what others have called the harmony of the spheres or the smile of God." Something, in other words, that "does not know time, history, before and after".[13]

Happiness, in other words, is a superior form of wisdom, detachment, imperturbability of the spirit, borne with lightness and a smile. Hesse was always an insatiable reader, a man of vast culture—classical and modern, philosophical and literary. Among the greatest authors, the one Hesse most loved was Goethe. But what Hesse sought in Goethe was the wisdom of the man. In an essay written for the centenary of Goethe's death at the request of his friend Romain Rolland, he asked himself why Goethe was so important to him, why he had always looked to him in every situation, even when he was impatient with a particular passage. What he particularly admired in Goethe was the wisdom of his old age, the detachment of certain late letters and poems, the rarefied atmosphere of the final version of *Faust*—a wisdom which went beyond fashions and trends, which was no longer either bourgeois or revolutionary or

47

classical; a wisdom which can also be found in the civilisations of India, China and Greece, because it is simply respect and love for life.

Our anxieties do not change and the times in which we live are no easier than those of Hesse. Our hopes for an era of peace have once again proved short-lived; the world is again threatened with wars and pervaded with a sense of insecurity and instability that has effects on the life of the individual. As an antidote to the ills of the world, Hesse does not propose a doctrine or a universal dogma; he asserts rather that the secret of life can be found in the individual's inner experience.

THE PATIENCE
OF THE TREE

THE LESSON OF NATURE

THERE IS AN AUTOBIOGRAPHICAL PIECE, which Hesse called *Childhood of the Magician* (the magician being, of course, himself), in which the writer recounts how, many years before, he had learnt the secrets of magic—his teachers had been the sun and the rain, the river and the woods, the insects that populate the earth and the birds that populate the sky. That was how things had been during his childhood, before his school years began. In his memory school remains an enemy, the implacable destroyer of all creativity, the leveller of all spontaneity. It is school that deprives the young protagonist of his novel *Beneath the Wheel*—a partial self-portrait—of the freedom to stroll along the river, the pleasure of going fishing and doing all the other carefree things which are done at that age. Hesse would hate school all his life. Instead, he had another great teacher, nature, from which he drew real lessons and to which he would remain for ever bound.

The last years of the nineteenth century and the first years of the twentieth have some affinities with our times, straddling as they did two centuries. Then, as now, the discoveries of science over the previous years were being increasingly applied and bringing about profound changes in customs and habits. People's aspirations changed too, as did the use they made of the land around them. In the last decades of the nineteenth century, the Germans, encouraged by a rate of growth that was among the highest in Europe, and anxious to take advantage of the potential riches that the new technologies placed within their reach, migrated in huge numbers from the countryside to the cities. When the Empire was born, in 1871, there were eight cities in Germany of more than one hundred thousand inhabitants; by the eve of the First World War there were forty-eight, and the population of Berlin quadrupled during the same period, reaching two million.

Like every great social phenomenon, urbanisation provoked opposing reactions. Starting in intellectual circles and then spreading among the upper middle classes, a feeling of aversion to cities grew up in Germany, a hatred of the metropolis encapsulated in the word *Großstadtfeindschaft*, which was to become a recurring motif in much twentieth-century German literature and art. It was nourished by a sense of nostalgia for a lifestyle untouched by industrialisation, a regret for the old unspoiled landscapes that had once existed, and for older forms of social organisation based on simplicity and solidarity—all themes to which the Germanic spirit has always been sensitive and which have solid roots in Romanticism.

Hesse belonged by family custom and cultural choice to this tradition. The silent landscapes of Southern Germany, the woods, rivers and lakes among which he was born and spent his childhood, had been, up until that point, less affected by the process of industrialisation that had substantially overtaken other areas of the Empire. There, the great changes in German society were only just beginning, the process of urban drift was not yet conspicuous, the countryside had not yet been transformed into suburbs, and the new metropolitan culture, identified above all with Berlin, had not yet taken off.

From his adolescence, Hesse placed himself firmly on the side of nature, a position he would maintain as he matured. All around him, in opposition to ways of life that were seen as increasingly alienating, new social groupings were springing up, all of which took nature as their ideal: the *Wandervögel* (migrating birds), a youth movement imbued with romantic dreams—comparable in some ways to the Scouts—which promoted a strong sense of group spirit and devoted itself to exploring the environment; the first followers of the anthroposophical theories of Rudolf Steiner, who tried, in contrast to the positivistic, mechanistic interpretation of reality, to fathom the secret laws of the cosmos and find in them an intimate harmony with man; and small alternative communities which proposed simply to create a model of life that resisted the trends prevalent in the society of their time. Of these communities, the best known and certainly the most eccentric was Monte Verità, above Ascona, in the canton of Ticino. Its heterogeneous membership was united by the common denominator of a profound disapproval of contemporary society and the authoritarian culture with which it was dominated. At Monte Verità there were anarchists and pacifists, whose motivation was clearly political in nature; there were those who aspired to a total liberation of the body and the senses and practised nudism and free dancing, those who advocated new health fads such as vegetarianism, teetotalism, non-smoking, homeopathy and other types of natural medicine, and those who were searching for new forms of truth in Eastern philosophy or in theosophy.

These were, as we can see, aspirations and tendencies quite similar to, if not identical with, certain beliefs and practices present in today's post-industrial society. Today, like then, the world is experiencing rapid and profound change and new modes of living and communicating. Today, even more than then, uncontrolled growth is endangering the natural balance and threatening resources that are part of everyone's birthright. Themes which a century ago might have appeared signs of eccentricity or hysteria, such as a passionate defence of the environment or the prioritising of laws governing the biosphere over those governing profits, have now become commonly accepted truths, both in principle and practice.

In the first decades of the twentieth century, Monte Verità was a seedbed for future ideas and a focus of curiosity and attraction for the whole of Europe. Intellectuals and artists—along with a certain number of rich idlers—flocked there to see what tomorrow's world might be like. Among them was Hesse, who knew one of the founders of the community—an eccentric sculptor, painter and preacher named Gusto Gräser—and saw it as an opportunity to experience group-living. His hostility to the rampant process of industrialisation then under way in Germany, his mistrust of big cities, and his lifelong predilection for small towns as yet untouched by progress certainly corresponded to some of the principles that were then spreading from Monte Verità to certain sectors of the European avant-garde. Without ever becoming one of its leading lights, Hesse did spend several months there in 1907—one of the reasons being that he had been recently drinking too much, as he sometimes did during periods of depression, and needed to dry out.

The desire to escape the pressures of modernity and find shelter in the natural world is already present in the novel *Peter Camenzind*, which, as we have seen, met with unexpected success, especially among the young. The reason for this success was surely that for Hesse, who was not yet thirty, and for many like him of a generation just coming to maturity, nature constituted an escape from everything unloved. The high mountains where Peter Camenzind wanders are pure and intact compared with the squalor of the cities; the skies are clear compared with the thick fogs of the plains; the air is silent compared with the hubbub rising from below. Nature has the colours of life and bestows them generously on men. Hesse is there to welcome them and make them his, just as those two great, passionate observers of nature, Vincent Van Gogh and Paul Gauguin, were doing at about the same time. In his novel, Hesse/Camenzind also talks of a pedagogical intention linked to the belief that nature is the true source of well-being and happiness: "I also wanted to teach men to find in a fraternal love for nature a source of joy, a current of life; I wanted to 'preach' the art of seeing, of exploring, of enjoying."[14] What upsets him is that men's thoughts are turning increasingly to current fashions and the mirage of novelty; that their minds are suffocated by scientific progress and their ears deafened by the noise of trains and cars. Throughout his life, through all his changing moods and tormented creative processes, nature, for Hesse, was a constant source of inspiration and a fundamental metaphor. Over time, of course, its meaning changed. At first it was a magical element, a place for games, the pure enchantment of adolescence. Then it lost the descriptive, impressionistic character it had in his youthful poetry and other works and gradually assumed an increasingly explicit symbolic function. The beauty of nature is sometimes used as a warning of the transitoriness of human existence, at other times its absolute authenticity is taken as a model of independence, an encouragement to reject laws that are not one's own, a sign of loyalty to oneself and one's own origins. And finally, nature mirrors the great, continual process of metamorphosis that constitutes the essence of the world, reflecting the transitoriness of all things and yet containing within itself the seeds of rebirth. It is a fully mature adult Hesse who says in one of his poems:

I have already died all deaths,
And I am going to die all deaths again,
Die the death of the wood in the tree,
Die the stone death in the mountain…
I will be born again, flowers
Tree and grass I will be born again,
Fish and deer, bird and butterfly.[15]

It sometimes happens that in old age, a sepia veil comes between our eyes and what we see. The shapes are unchanged and perfectly recognisable, but the colours drain away and the brown of time takes their place. Something similar happened to Hesse—as he aged, nature assumed a different dimension. In his late poetry, duller tones dominate, the faded hues of autumn and the greys of winter; the branches are bare, the earth is barren. The colours have gone, and nature is now in tune with the final season of a man's life.

WATER, AIR, EARTH, FIRE

H ESSE'S VISION OF NATURE is the result of an unusual syncretism. It combines the Christian mysticism of Saint Francis and his teachings on the brotherhood of all animate things, Goethe's belief that even the smallest thing is governed by universal laws and in this sense encapsulates the whole, and, finally, after a certain point in Hesse's life, the message of the Vedas, the sacred texts of Hinduism—that the individual soul and the universal soul are one and the same. So not only every living creature, but also things apparently without life, can think and speak, feel pain and pleasure, win and lose like human beings: "Mountains, lake, storm and sun were my friends; they told me stories and educated me and for a long time were dearer and more familiar to me than any human being and human destiny."[16]

Clouds occupy a prime position in Hesse's symbolism. They appear and disappear without leaving a trace, their forms are changeable and transitory, and they are elusive and uncontaminated. Man can neither reach nor disturb their purity, his technology is powerless against them, and he can only gaze at them from afar. They are the first and most elementary manifestation of the divine.

Water has the mobility and immateriality of clouds, but is closer to men. If clouds appear particularly in Hesse's youthful writings, water is his companion throughout his life. Indeed, given that he spent all his life near water, on the banks of rivers or the shores of lakes, it is hardly surprising that there are barely any of his longer works in which water does not appear in one way or another.

Water reflects the outside world. It also reflects the human personality and is therefore an instrument of analysis, observation and listening, which provokes questions, thoughts and omens. When Hesse undertakes the exploration of himself he finds in water an archetype of his unconscious; when he goes deeper into the Indian tradition and then, with the *Tao te ching*, into the ancient wisdom of China, he again finds in water a model of reference for human conduct. In *Siddhartha*, a central text in his mystical pilgrimage, it is by performing the repetitive daily act of ferrying travellers across the river that his protagonist becomes aware of the meaning of man's destiny. Siddhartha meditates on the course of his life by the river; he listens to the river and knows that it is there that the brilliant simplicity of the answer awaits him.

Hesse loved the metaphysical quality of air and water. When it came to the most physical of the elements, the earth, what he felt was gratitude, because the plants take their sustenance and stability from it. Of all plants, he most loved trees, and, of all trees, the isolated ones, in which he felt a connection to his own destiny and that of man, and which recur frequently in his writings. Solitary trees are warriors who fight their battles alone: "The world rustles in their branches, their roots sink into the infinite and yet are not lost in it, but pursue with all their strength a single aim—to realise the law that is innate in them; to bring their form to perfection; to represent themselves."[17] The fulfilment of one's own destiny is indeed a solitary task. A man seeks out his own inclinations, alone; it is alone that, with his feet firmly planted on the earth and his senses on the alert in the attempt to see and listen to nature, he constructs his life. Alone, he has sufficient strength to complete his own cycle, and, if he loses his way and his confidence in himself, looking at the trees reminds him that salvation does not come from others but from himself; that his homeland is not in some place in the world, but within himself. When despair assails him and he does not know in which direction to go, says Hesse, the tree transmits its lesson to him: "Hush, now! Look at me! Life is not easy, life is not difficult."[18]

57

This silent, patient lesson from the trees was one that Hesse tried to convey to the many readers who turned to him for advice on how to overcome their doubts and uncertainties, their inability to decide which path to follow. Hesse did not attempt to tell them which, among the many possibilities, was the way that each person should choose. Nor would he try to tell each person how to distinguish between what was right and what was wrong. The one thing he was able to say with certainty was the same thing that the tree told him—that there is no point in adapting ourselves to external rules that we do not share; there is no point in looking for short cuts or labouring under the illusion that others can make our journey for us. To a confused young man who, like so many others, had written to him asking for help, he wrote back that one should "say yes to one's self, one's own isolation, one's own feelings, one's own destiny."[19]

Nothing in nature is superfluous or useless. The lowliest animal and the most insignificant stone have as much value as a forest or a mountain, because every living creature, every inanimate thing, is the bearer of a message. Hesse, unlike Goethe, whom he admired so much, was not a scholar of the natural world. He had no interest in subdivisions or classifications. Nor did he experiment, except through his daily practice. He loved clouds because they were clouds and because of the thoughts they gave rise to. He loved water because it was water and because he saw in it his own destiny. He loved trees and plants because they helped him to live and survive.

He also loved fire, as we shall see, because from the ashes, mixed with earth, life is reborn. Air, water, earth and fire were, in their way, his teachers.

WALKING—A THERAPY FOR BODY AND MIND

A S WE HAVE ALREADY SEEN, Hesse was not a great traveller. He travelled in his youth, especially to Italy, and made a single long journey, to the Far East, which, by and large, did not fill him with enthusiasm. But he did not really feel the need for new horizons; he had no great desire to see exotic landscapes for himself, or to become acquainted with the great cities of the world. On the other hand, he was a tireless walker over short distances. The figure of the romantic wanderer, crossing hills, valleys, woods and villages on foot, is among his favourite images and recurs in many of his works. In *Knulp*, a fine story inspired by Joseph von Eichendorff, the most romantic of the Romantic poets and certainly one of those whom Hesse most loved, the main character is a wanderer who lives from hand to mouth, constantly moving with the rain and with the sun, spending one night in a tavern and the next in a peasant house. Time passes. He ages prematurely, and with age comes fatigue and illness. But Knulp continues walking and wondering about the meaning of life. He dies at the end of the story, struggling through a snowstorm.

During his boyhood in Calw, Hesse had got into the habit of leaving his house whenever he could to wander in the surrounding area. The destination was less important than movement in itself, walking for one's own pleasure in the open air—one wood, from this point of view, was as good as any other. This love of aimless wandering had continued through his adolescence and young manhood—we just have to read the passionate description in his book *Wandering* of a long excursion he made from the Swiss Alps to Lake Como, through silent villages and solitary roads, talking about simple things with the simple people of the place, perhaps humming a popular song he had just learnt, with joy in his heart.

Hesse's journeys to Italy in the first years of the century were, in a sense, an exception. One way or another, whether he liked it or not, he was forced to become a tourist. He tried to avoid this fate as much as possible—he avoided the usual itineraries and the sight of other tourists repelled him. He did, admittedly, travel by train—although in third-class carriages—visit cities of artistic interest and spend time in museums. But he always preferred villages and long rambles on foot, and as soon as he could he would set off at random. He found the warmth and good humour of the Italians infectious; he looked at the landscapes and compared them with those the old masters painted in their altarpieces. He was not dismayed by the modesty of his lodgings, nor did he feel uncomfortable about the fact that he knew little of the language. His itineraries were often unpredictable—the shores of Lake Trasimeno, filled with reeds and birds, the little Umbrian towns perched on their inaccessible hills. They, too, like the walls and the churches, were, for him, as much part of 'nature' as the lakes and streams.

When, just before the outbreak of war, his Italian travels came to an end, his love of walking in the open air, looking at the plants by the side of the road, following the course of a brook, led Hesse to undertake excursions that were more confined in terms of distance—between the cantons of eastern Switzerland—but just as delightful. In the story called *Wandering*, he tells of mountains and streams, peasant houses and country graveyards, farms and chapels, in a prose that alternates felicitously with poetry.

Whether in Italy or in Switzerland, whether he is going through a village and stopping to talk to an old man sitting in a doorway or walking through a fir wood in the mountains and stopping to pick a jonquil, what Hesse is looking for is, at one and the same time, rules and freedom. Not the rules imposed by men, but the great absolute rules of nature—Hesse knows well that the peasant world, which he had discovered on his excursions, has its laws, too. They are, however, laws dictated not by the will of men, but by the cycle of the days and the turning of the seasons; the rhythms of tilling the soil and harvesting the crops. Accepting these laws does not mean losing one's freedom. Because it was freedom, within the great laws that govern the world, that Hesse was really searching for—he says it openly, even with a certain naivety, when he crosses the border between two cantons: "How good it is to cross these borders! The wanderer is in many ways a primitive man just as the nomad is more primitive than the peasant ... If there were many people who had the same contempt for borders as I have, there would be no more wars or blocs. There is nothing more odious than borders, nothing more stupid than borders."[20]

Moving about and crossing borders, even the abstract borders of a peaceful Swiss canton, had the symbolic meaning of a conquest of freedom. But movement did not only have a symbolic value. For a time, Hesse had thought that he would find a cure for his restlessness and anxiety—and perhaps did, in fact, find it—by running away from home or school. The idea that physical exercise ensures not only the well-being of the body but also that of the mind is, in any case, as old as the world. As it was for Goethe, whom he regarded as an inimitable paragon of good-living and wisdom, so for Hesse movement was eternally necessary, and walking its simplest and most direct expression. *Wandern*, then, is not only walking, it is an intimate involvement with nature and the world, an enlargement of one's own knowledge, and a stimulus to thought and creativity.

Even when he grew older, and was tormented by migraines and aching bones, he would regard walking as a necessary prerequisite for a sense of balance, and would try and set aside a time each day for it. The longer excursions he had once undertaken gave way to shorter walks, and he would stop more often at an open-air tavern or sit on a bench to look at the surrounding hills. There is a photograph taken by his son Martin when he was already in his sixties, in which we see him, in a pair of wide trousers and a straw hat on his head, against the background of the snow-covered Alps, walking, with the gait of a boy, towards some village or other.

Physical movement is linked to the knowledge and love of natural things. Goethe said that the study of nature, of whatever kind and whatever the point of departure, detaches us from ourselves, directs our intellectual capacities to the outside world, and leads us to reflect on real, concrete phenomena—in short, it constitutes an education in reality which both helps us and gives us pleasure.

This is the crux of the matter—nature helps us to look within and understand ourselves and to look without and understand the laws that govern the world. Many modern studies of the human mind, in disciplines such as psychology, medicine or philosophy itself, have adopted these principles.

Hesse's originality lies not only in the fact that, as we shall see, he conceived of a path where elements of the classical and Christian traditions combine with elements of Eastern philosophy, leading to a unified conception which seems to respond to the deepest needs of certain levels of contemporary society, but above all in the fact that he understood the metaphysical aspect of some forms of physical activity and advocated their therapeutic value in dealing with the disorders and anxieties of man's psyche. Nothing better reflects this insight than Hesse's passionate love of gardens.

PLANTS AND FLOWERS

F OR MANY PEOPLE, especially in the middle classes of the industrialised world, the garden is their main connection with nature, the main way they have to get close to it, learn to know it, and make it their friend. So it was for Hesse—his love of gardens went so deep, he devoted so much of his time and his thoughts to them, and wrote so often about them, that it could be said with some justification that they profoundly influenced his artistic and human personality.

He was nine years old when his mother entrusted him with a small flower bed on the slope behind their house in Calw. There he had his first experience of the natural world, and he has left us an affectionate description of that child's garden. Like many children, Hesse was not fond of half-shades, but loved to be surrounded by bright, intense colours. He preferred, as he himself said, simpler, humbler, more rustic species. These were tastes that he would keep into his adult life, as he would demonstrate in all the gardens he had during his lifetime.

The first garden was the one at Gaienhofen. When Hesse left his temporary home, the peasant house he had rented in that small village on Lake Constance, far from the main roads, he bought a plot of land just outside the village, built a house and surrounded it with a large garden. As always, he gives us an accurate description accompanied by a number of detailed drawings. At first he planted a kitchen garden to feed his small family and exercise his talents as a grower. But, as there was no lack of space, he soon decided to grow flowers as well, especially his favourites, sunflowers, which would always keep him company over the years—flowers that are perfect in their form and in their bright colour which inspires happiness, flowers that imitate the sun and follow it on its celestial journey. Hesse did not, of course, neglect the growing of food, but the needs of the household were few and the seeds he planted provided simple but substantial nourishment. Among the flowers were bright dahlias, humble nasturtiums, pendulous fuchsias, triumphant zinnias, along with roses, carnations and mallows. Hesse always appreciated hot, almost harsh colours— reds, oranges, yellows which, like the sun, cheer the mind and warm the heart.

In his preference for brightly-coloured plants, Hesse was a child of his time—in the first decades of the twentieth century, middle-class gardens in continental Europe were based on the Victorian model, but with the addition of some elements of spontaneity and rusticity, as propounded by English theoreticians like Gertrud Jekyll. The absence of formal concerns or architectural pretensions typical of the cottage garden coincides fully with Hesse's choices and with his predilection for bright colours that keep the mind alert and transmit energy and vitality.

The years spent in Gaienhofen with Mia Bernoulli were not easy years for either of them, and they were both experiencing mental problems. During this difficult period, the garden was for Hesse a constant source of little joys—watching the plants grow and the flowers open, toiling away at the modest vegetables in the kitchen garden. Even when he left Gaienhofen and moved to Bern, to a house that had belonged to a painter friend who had recently died, Hesse was surrounded by a garden, though of a very different kind from that of the rustic house on Lake Constance. That had been a young garden, tended by Hesse according to his whims, rich in colours and poor in ordered patterns. This was almost a park, with a long history behind it, laid out in an aristocratic fashion, with a fountain, avenues of old trees and high, carefully trimmed hedges. Hermann and

Mia now had three sons—for the two of them, trying in vain to escape the solitude that lowered their spirits, life in Bern did not bring relief, but for their sons the garden became a place of mystery and enchantment. Hesse transfigured it in a beautiful story, *The House of Dreams*, which unfortunately was never finished even though he worked on it for a long time and considered some parts of it from a stylistic point of view as being among the best things he had ever done. In the story, an old man named Neander skilfully tends his garden. Neander has seen many things in his life, travelled, met many people, had important posts and received honours. Now he is old, and he decides that the time has come to leave everything behind him and pass from action to contemplation.

In drawing this character, Hesse was inspired by the figure of a Taoist sage. Neander's decision is not an act of abdication or rejection; it is the final gesture of a man's life, a slow leave-taking of the things of this world, the moment when the threads of life begin to loosen and the few essential things are gathered together before the point of no return. The journey towards this ultimate phase takes place in a large garden of majestic old trees filled with birds, high lilac bushes and luxuriant roses. A garden, says the son of the story's main character, which is like a fairy tale; and old Neander, has the role that magicians have in fairy tales. The seasons go round, the garden changes as they change, and these changes, in which memories alternate with the anticipation of death, sum up the course of a man's life. Neander looks up and sees the outlines of high mountains beyond the plants that grow, bloom and wither. He knows that the struggle is over, that the time of renunciation and an unquenchable nostalgia has come: "Since he had crossed the summits of life and had started penetrating the valley of long shadows, his thoughts had renounced the thought of death. The country from which he had come and the country towards which he was going were one and the same."[21] This is the profoundly consolatory thought which daily work in the garden, or at least as much as an old man's hands and legs will allow, inspires in Neander—that there is no separation between life and death. Death is the return to a homeland, a *Heimat*, abandoned at the moment of birth.

One of Hesse's favourite Romantic poets, Novalis, said that whatever the poet looks for, he will find nowhere but in his own soul. So, too, old Neander, in the plants he cultivates, the earth he tills and fertilises, the thoughts the garden arouses in him and the reflections it suggests to him, finds only himself.

And yet the garden is also something else. Despite his idiosyncratic and completely ungregarious life, Hesse was not, as we have seen, indifferent to what was happening around him in the world. However reluctantly, he kept a dismayed eye on the transformations and tragedies of the century in which he lived. His gardens were the product of a meditative individual state, but, at the same time, they were also the response of an intellectual to an era of bloody wars and social upheaval. A green space created by man became, both practically and symbolically, an oasis of stability and order, linked to the cyclical rhythms of nature, compared with the spaces of instability and disorder that man was creating with his hunger for conquest and his will to destroy.

In his choice of places to live, Hesse took a series of small steps from north to south, gradually distancing himself from the Germanic world in favour of more southern landscapes and accents—from Tübingen in the Black Forest to Basle, then the shores of Lake Constance and from there to Bern. In 1919, soon after the end of the war, he left German Switzerland and settled by himself in the canton of Ticino, first temporarily in a peasant house, then in Montagnola, in the curious Casa Camuzzi, surrounded by a garden full of splendid old trees. The climate was mild and there were luxuriant climbing plants on the tree trunks. Two of these trees were particularly dear to him—a big magnolia, which astonished him every time with the extent of its flowering, and a Judas tree, which enchanted him first with its pink springtime hues and then with the purplish colours of its autumn pods. Hesse recalled the end of the Judas tree in some moving pages written some years later, after his friend Hugo Ball had died and he had accompanied the body on a grey rainy day. The death of the tree came shortly after the death of his friend. He saw it torn down on a storm-tossed night, its massive trunk broken and a gaping hole in the ground where its roots had been. This death appeared to him more mysterious and unjust than that of his friend, who, Hesse believed, had attained peace—death had perhaps been the fulfilment of his cycle, perhaps even something he had obscurely wished for. The tree, of course, did not want to die; it had been there until a short time earlier, strong and vital, ready to blossom once again. Now, in its shattered state, only nothingness awaited it.

In Montagnola, Hesse had two gardens. The first, that of Casa Camuzzi, he regarded as a companion in his solitude and a key to interpreting the world—the outlines of the trees he could see from his window took the place of friends and of his absent family. But it was a garden that Hesse merely looked at, not one he had constructed and created. Like the bizarre house he lived in, it was a place to which he was grateful for having welcomed him, but which he never felt belonged to him. His second garden at Montagnola, on the other hand, played a fundamental role in his life, both physically and spiritually.

By the beginning of the 1930s, Hesse was a well-known writer and a man of mature years. Thanks to the generosity of his friend Hans C Bodmer, he had a new house commensurate with his growing fame as a man of letters and *maître à penser*. It was a large house above the village, with a lovely view of the surrounding hills. Around it there was a vast area of land, more than one hectare, on a steep slope. This is the place that became the garden of his life, and would remain so until his death thirty years later. He devoted enormous care to it and saw it as a measure of his relationship with the world. He began by improving the rocky soil, enriching it with compost and manure, developed an existing spring, built low walls, laid out paths and, on the edge of the wood, constructed a field for that most rustic of games, bowls.

The garden at Gaienhofen had had the metaphysical function of negating modernity, exalting solitude and asserting the superiority of individual choices over those of the mass, and, at the same time, the eminently physical function of a field of action on which to lavish his own energies, raw material for a simple and direct creative activity. To these practical and symbolic values, the garden of Montagnola added another, which was the result of the passing years—it became a therapeutic instrument which revealed and cured the ills of the body and soothed the anxieties of the mind through the intimate daily involvement of the life of man with the life of nature. Gardening, alternating with writing, relieved the ills that age brought with it—his frequent migraines, the pains in his eyes and limbs. At the same time, says Hesse, it encouraged "meditation, the weaving of the threads of imagination, the concentrating of states of mind."[22]

In Hesse's day, a rejection of sophistication and artifice and a taste for simple, natural things were still a rare, almost eccentric, individual choice. More than half-a-century would pass before this choice would start to spread through the wider strata of society, until it became a necessity for many, a fashion for others. Hesse, however, had not been the first and was not the only one to talk of such things. He had had illustrious predecessors—philosophers, moralists, essayists and novelists. The most famous of the novelists, of course, was Tolstoy, the older Tolstoy in particular, who had preached simplicity and humility, and himself set an example that was almost excessive.

Hesse was quite different by nature, but the taste for a certain degree of poverty in his life never left him. In his youth, he had loved stopping at the most modest Italian tavern and talking to the tavernkeeper, and this was a habit he kept into old age. In his comfortable, spacious house in Montagnola, he left the larger rooms and the terrace with its splendid view for his guests, and chose a modest area near the stables for himself, which he also made the command post, as it were, of his garden.

It was here that Hesse began his day of activity—digging and fertilising, watering and weeding. Once again, he pursued simplicity—the dog roses and their red autumn berries, the sunflowers which, as at Gaienhofen, lit up the slope like splashes of light, the fruit trees and the vegetables in the kitchen garden. This patient, often laborious work was the subject of a long poem in hexameters on the model of Virgil's *Georgics* and *Eclogues*, entitled *Hours in the Garden*, written in 1933 for the sixtieth birthday of his sister Adele. In it, every gesture, every step is described with both the precision of a gardening manual and the sensitivity of a poet.

The day starts early, with a careful, loving look around at the state of the garden, to see where nature requires his intervention. When he gets down to work, Hesse recounts in detail how he pulls out the weeds, prunes the trees, which weaker plants he supports with poles, which bent branches he tries to prop up. He takes care that each thing should be done with the maximum economy and, as far as possible, with the means he has at his disposal—the string he uses is taken from the parcels of books his publishers send him; the books themselves, those unnecessary ones which would take up space pointlessly on the shelves, are laid down without any compunction instead of stones to be a base for new paths. His gestures are slow. Hesse always chooses the longest way, trying not to skip the intermediate stages, to respect the principal of continuity. He alone prepares most of the substances that nourish his garden—he burns the foliage, grass and roots he has extracted from the earth, sifts the ashes and scatters it equally over the plants that need it. As he works, he thinks of the frantic life of the world around him, the relentless onslaught of technologies, which follow and overtake one another in an obsessive attempt to gain time. Hesse is closing the circle of his existence, between his present old age and his past youth—because between past and present, spring and autumn, there is no conflict and no split. The garden knows nothing of past or future, it is always the same because it breaks down and is recomposed, dies and is eternally reborn. Like the river in *Siddhartha* it is a symbol of uninterrupted flow.

No different from the flow of water is the burning of fire. There is a drawing by his friend Günther Böhmer that shows him burning grass and dry branches, leaning towards the flames with his arm outstretched. Since ancient times, fire has had a twofold symbolic value, both destructive and regenerative. Hesse is attracted above all by the latter. He sees fire as a symbol of regeneration—from fire comes ash and from ash comes new life, which in turn becomes ash and then again life. When he sets fire to the shrubs in his garden, collects the ashes and scatters them over the plants he is growing, Hesse feels that he is performing the function of a priest officiating over a process of mystical union with nature. Fire, he writes in *Hours in the Garden*, has, among its other meanings, also that of a chemical-symbolic act of worship of the divinity and represents the return of the multiplicity of creatures and things in the world to a primal unity.

This, in fact, is one of the central points of his thought. It is also, as we shall see later when we look at the influence on Hesse of Eastern philosophies, one of the most intimately consolatory points. In an essay inspired by one of the most ambiguous creatures a gardener can observe in his work environment, a caterpillar that has become a butterfly (the essay is actually called *On Butterflies*), Hesse puts forward the idea that the changeable nature of butterflies reflects the idea of a great, hidden unity at the basis of the manifold; a single primal mother responsible for all births. Instead of amusing us, the infinite variety of forms should lead us on our infinite, nostalgic search for the unique contained within the manifold, the weak that conquers the strong, the flexible that defeats the resistant, and all the differences and contrasts which make up the balance of nature. This was how his friend Böhmer saw Hesse—squatting like a Chinese, handling the remains of a vegetable world on the verge of decomposition and preparing to transform it into a source of life. Together with the wisdom he derived from the classics, Hesse's position, his vision of the world, also included the Taoist *wu wei*, the desire not to hinder the course of things, to let things happen without interfering, to accept that what occurs happens without claiming to improve or teach anything. This is how he expresses it:

> *While the world is ruled by coarser, yet more violent forces,*
> *Wisdom remains alchemy and diversion for the wise.*
> *And so, let us be modest, even in an age of oppression*
> *Let us set against the course of the world that calm of the soul*
> *The old one praised and aspired to, let us do good.*
> *Without a thought of changing the world, even so it will pay.*[23]

The pleasure a garden can give the person who tends it or even the person who only admires it, the enchantment we derive from the colour of a flower, the intoxication that comes from the scent of a narcissus or a hyacinth—all this has been said many times, before and after Hesse. The affinity between the plant and man, between the flower and his soul, is another theme that literature has frequently made its own. The great essayist and connoisseur of gardens Rudolf Borchardt, born the same year as Hesse, and author of the deservedly famous *The Passionate Gardener*, which can quite rightly be considered the one gardening book closest to great literature, put it in this way—the flower is the commonest of all similes in every language and in all parts of the world because it is the perfect symbol of human things, "what we have, and what we had".[24]

What is different and, in a sense, unique in Hesse's message is not so much the fact that he compares the life of man and the cycle of the plant, as the human and relieving side of that message. It is the fact that, through his own life, he offered the garden as a model for surviving the ills of the world, be they public or private.

In a letter from 1933, the fatal year in which Germany laid the foundations of its own downfall, Hesse wrote to a friend that the only way he could react to the news coming out of Germany was to devote all his efforts to working in his garden. What emerged from Germany in those days was a torrent of words, a great disorder behind which there could be detected, as Hesse clearly saw, the sinister order that was yet to come.

The garden, where "the entire simple cycle of life that so much preoccupies men and which all religions interpret with veneration, takes place unambiguously, rapidly and in silence",[25] is not only a refuge from the disorders of the mind and the ills of the body, it is also a shield with which the individual can protect himself from the barbarism ravaging the world.

Gardening is hard work. The gardener's movements, Hesse tells us, are simple, humble and repetitious. The genuflexion a person tending to a small plant has to make alludes to something religious, to the celebration of a cult. Repetition gives pleasure; humility gives joy. In these statements, we hear the echoes of a Franciscan mysticism that Hesse had known in his youth and of an Eastern mysticism he came to know in later years. Work and meditation, the expression of the individual and the representation of the cosmos are, in reality, one and the same. And it takes patience—one should not be under any illusion that complicated tools or expensive materials can replace the work of man in this process with its profound double meaning. This is a warning against excessive ambition, pointless sophistication, the sham of those 'instant gardens' popularised by a certain kind of modern horticulture; it is a call to let time flow and for everyone to adapt to that rhythm, as it is the natural rhythm of men and things.

THE VIRTUES OF SLOWNESS

T HE PAGES IN WHICH HESSE DEMONSTRATED, through his own
personal experience, his knowledge of gardens, are among
the richest and most original he ever wrote. Without doubt, they
show, as does all his thought, the clear influence of Romanticism.
Certain symbolic images of Romantic literature—brooks, foliage, birds, springs—recur frequently in both his poetry and his
prose. But Hesse is not on the lookout for virgin, unspoilt nature,
but rather for nature of which man is a part and an instrument; not the wilderness, but the kitchen garden and the flower
garden; not enchantment and astonishment, but the sense of
belonging and harmony and, through these, happiness. A happiness which is not static or sudden, not a miraculous gift that
descends to man from above, but an active, patient achievement
which comes from below.

We touch here on a key point of Hesse's thought and one of
the things that make him a profoundly 'modern' thinker. This
particular Hessian 'happiness' is the product of slowness. In
a historical period like that in which he lived, in which ever
newer and more rapid technological developments gave rise to
the belief that the whole world can be reduced to the brain of
man and his creations—in this respect, a period not so very
different from our own—Hesse lays claim, not to the speed of
progress, but the slowness of nature. Today, he would be on
the side of the 'slow food' movement, set up in opposition to
the omnipresence of fast food, or among those who prefer a
country road to a highway.

Observation requires time. The careful observation of the
passing seasons, the perpetual cycle of death and rebirth, the

constant metamorphosis of which man and nature are part, is not something that takes a day, or even a year, but a whole life. It makes our old age and the thought of our death less dreadful, says Hesse, because it allows us to understand, in so far as it is given to man to do so, that everything, even old age and death, is included in the great universal order. It is pointless to believe, or pretend to believe, that one can free oneself from either of them: "Time passes and wisdom remains. It changes its forms and its rituals, but is based always on the same foundation— on the integration of man with nature, in the rhythm of the cosmos."[26]

METAMORPHOSIS OF A GARDEN

TIME, then, passes and, while wisdom remains, things change, die and are reborn in another form. In the same way, the thought of Hesse remains current, while his gardens have been transformed, have died and been partly reborn. The great garden of his house in Montagnola, which he created himself and where he worked passionately for three decades, was sold some time ago to a wealthy industrialist and entry is forbidden to visitors. Local people say that it has greatly changed since then. If you peer in from outside, you get the impression that little of the simple rustic character that Hesse gave it has remained—instead it has acquired an opulence and dignity in keeping with its present owner. Conversely, the first garden Hesse created, on Lake Constance, passed from hand to hand and was severely neglected, before being bought, some years ago, by an enthusiastic couple who, with patience, botanical expertise and a careful analysis of documents, have been attempting to restore it to the state in which Hesse left it, making use of his sketches and descriptions, reintroducing the plants of that time and even planting varieties of vegetables which existed a century ago and which have now mostly disappeared.

Far from where Hesse lived, in the places in Italy that he loved and walked across in his youth, on the borders of Umbria and Tuscany, I have created a garden inspired by him and his vision of man and nature. This garden of bushes, berries and simple flowers with strong, vibrant colours such as he preferred, draws on his therapeutic message and, by reviving, through reading, not only his teachings but those of his great masters, from Goethe to Lao-Tzu, encourages visitors to look at life with serenity and awareness.

THE WAY TO THE EAST

A WORLD OF BOOKS

I F WE LOOK AT THE PHOTOGRAPHS OF HESSE from the different periods of his long life, we will note that he is often shown on his own, with a stern look and a touch of haughty detachment. As time passes, the thoughts and doubts that mark out his journey through life leave increasingly deep marks on his face, while his height and almost unnatural thinness help to give him an enigmatic, solitary intensity. But in other images—the most frequent and the most beautiful—we see him with a book in his hand or surrounded by books in his library, bent over a desk piled high with books while he writes with a pen or a typewriter. Hesse, who had hated school as a young boy and at fourteen ran away and was pursued by the police across fields and woods, became a passionate and tireless reader in his young manhood and remained so for the rest of his life. It might even be said that books, more than people, were his great companions.

His reading was based on personal vocation and choice, not discipline or obedience. What most contributed to his love of books was his maternal grandfather's huge library, which included thousands of volumes and countless manuscripts from the four corners of the world. There was half-light and silence, and a trace of pipe smoke in the air. Over this mountain of knowledge his grandfather kept watch, raising his eyes from his studies to watch with a detached smile whenever little Hermann crept in shyly, unable to resist the spell of the place.

Hesse described that example of eclectic, universal wisdom in this lovely passage: "The noble, powerful old man with his long white beard was omniscient, more important than father and mother, and in possession of quite other treasures—not only did the Indian toy god and all the other carved and painted and magically consecrated things belong to him ... but he himself was a magician, a wise man, a sage."[27]

Hesse's library at Montagnola was not all that different from his grandfather's. Here, too, there was half-light, silence and a persistent trace, not of pipe smoke but cigar smoke. Here, too, shelves full of volumes from every part of the world covered the walls from floor to ceiling. The books of literature and poetry were carefully arranged by nationality, but there were also many works of philosophy, psychology and psychoanalysis, history and religion.

Every great intellectual is asked, sooner or later, which, in his judgement, are the ten or fifty or hundred greatest books ever written. Hesse answered this question in a short essay from 1929, entitled *A Library of World Literature*. His choice is highly personal and not at all objective, it makes no claim to exhaustiveness, neglects some great names, and almost completely ignores modern and contemporary writers. What Hesse looks for in books is not emotion but wisdom, he does not read to pass the time but to find the keys to time. His selection reflects a vision of what, according to him, the true aim of culture should be— to lead to a "broadening of our consciousness, an enrichment of our potential for life and joy."[28]

Hesse loved the great classical texts of antiquity, which have stood the test of time and can no longer grow old. He loved Socrates, the wisest of wise men, and found in his idea of 'virtue' the same wisdom as with the ancient Chinese and Indians. He came from a deeply religious family and the Bible, the Gospels and other Christian writings were part of his intellectual development. He felt close to the medieval mystics, Saint Augustine, and the legends of the saints, in particular Saint Francis and certain figures of Protestant mysticism like Jakob Böhme.

This, then, was his library—all the great European literatures were present, but most space was taken up by German literature, especially its greatest period, from the middle of the eighteenth century to the middle of the nineteenth century, the Classical and Romantic eras. Goethe, who not only had a complete grounding in the European humanistic tradition but also dared to explore the East and drew from it not only poetic inspiration, but also lessons to be learnt, remained his prime model.

Even a superficial look at Hesse's bookshelves would reveal, however, an essential element of his personality and thought that was not common for a European writer of the time—the central place taken by the great texts of Indian and Chinese wisdom. The library at Montagnola belonged to his mature years and was completed in old age. It encapsulated a long intellectual journey, at once rigorous and bold, which led him gradually to reconnect with an East familiar from his childhood, his grandfather's memories and his father's stories; an East that was not picturesque but contemplative, not rich in adventures but filled with metaphors and wisdom.

INDIA

T HE INTEREST WE HAVE IN A DISTANT LAND and culture, such as India might be for a European mind, is almost always based on journeys we have taken or on the stories and impressions of others who have made such journeys themselves. Today, in the age of mass tourism, especially among the young, India has become an almost inescapable cultural destination. In other forms, that has already happened before. There have been times in European history when there were sudden waves of enthusiasm for the East that were not too dissimilar from those of today, although on a smaller scale. With the opening of the Suez Canal, which after the voyage of Columbus was man's greatest step towards globalisation, travelling to India to escape from a society that identified only with progress became a widespread fashion among educated minds of Wilhelmine Germany. Many German writers, whose names are now forgotten, went to India between the end of the nineteenth century and the first decades of the twentieth century, often commissioned by publishers, to gather their impressions and then recount them to readers avid for exoticism. Hesse, too, as we have seen, went to the East to see if the idea of it that he had in his mind, thanks to his readings and the family stories, corresponded to the reality.

We know that things did not work out that way. Hesse was a conscientious traveller—he made the required excursions in Sumatra, saw butterflies in Ceylon, went to the bazaar and even, twice, to a theatre in Malaysia; he suffered from the heat and was a little seasick. Perhaps the Asia that most impressed him was the Asia he saw in a dream when he fell asleep in a cinema of Singapore. "We are going to Asia, he said to himself in the dream; and they were already there."[29] In reality, Hesse was in search of India, but the cruise he took with his painter friend did not take him to India, but to the coastal areas of South-East Asia. Subsequently he gave the book in which he collected his travel impressions together with a few poems and various reflections the title *From India*.

His journey may not have brought him close to the East, but it did not distance him from it. He simply put aside the idea that there were models of social coexistence and daily life there that could be viable alternatives to those in the West. But he continued with his reading, even though the word 'India' would always remain intentionally vague for him—for example, in an essay written fourteen years later, which he entitled *Nostalgia for India*, his observations were inspired by two books published some time earlier in Germany, one about Sumatra and the other about Ceylon, which we now call Sri Lanka. In other words, it was not the geographical, the anthropological or even, strictly speaking, the historical East that interested Hesse. His India and his East were and would always remain abstractions, places of the mind. A good example of this is a long, enigmatic story which has the word 'East' in the title and which Hesse wrote almost twenty years after having gone there. In *Journey to the East*, all traces of his personal experience have gone, and the whole text is a mysterious, fascinating metaphor. A dense column of men and women are walking eastwards; we know nothing of their point of departure and little of the places they pass through, because, says Hesse, "this procession of believers and disciples had always and incessantly been moving towards the East, towards the Home of Light. Throughout the centuries it had been on the way, towards light and wonder, and each member, each group, indeed our whole host and its great pilgrimage, was only a wave in the eternal stream of human beings, of the eternal strivings of the human spirit towards the East, towards Home."[30]

But what then was this India, this East towards which no boat goes, and for which no train leaves, which can only be reached by looking into oneself and which perhaps no one will ever reach? Hesse was not the only writer to try and provide an answer. One such was his contemporary, the writer and essayist Hermann Keyserling, a lucid writer and essayist, who knew India well, with his *Travel Diary of a Philosopher*. Another was Stefan Zweig, in an inspired story—*The Eyes of My Brother, For Ever*. Many other writers of the period could be mentioned. Nobody, though, embarked on the search for a new truth in the East with the passionate consistency of Hesse, or left such clear traces of it on his own work. No one, above all, drew from Eastern thought such a persuasive, comforting message to anyone searching for a way to happiness.

What drove Hesse to venture into Indian culture was not the temptation to follow the example of the many who had preceded him on that road, let alone to imitate, as he himself wrote, the fashionable lady who buys a bronze Buddha and three volumes of his *Discourses* to go with it. The stimulus, as so often for Hesse, was intellectual rather than physical. What aroused his interest were the writings of certain thinkers, like Arthur Schopenhauer, who integrated some principles of Indian spirituality into their vision of the world. Another factor may have been the sometimes obscure and tortuous discussions of theosophy at Monte Verità. What is certain is that Hesse immersed himself in the reading of Eastern texts, knew the old Indian fables, and became familiar with the yoga aphorisms of Patanjali and with the *Kama Sutra*.

In *A Library of World Literature*, Hesse mentions the three texts that had the greatest influence on his intellectual development—the *Discourses* of Buddha, the *Upanishads*, and the *Bhagavad Gita*. From the *Discourses* of Buddha he derived his interest in meditation and self-exploration, an acceptance of the precariousness of things and an awareness that the world is in constant transformation. What seduced him in Buddha was the mental silence, the smile, the forgiveness, the impassive resolution and the impassive kindness. In Buddhism, he found detachment, and in that extraordinary collection of aphorisms, maxims, hymns and precepts known as the *Upanishads*, he discovered the way to overcome the dualism which marks every moment of existence and to configure a single principle in the world. If all things have the same origin and the same destiny, if everything that exists amounts to one single thing, then even the great categories of good and evil, right and wrong, the great moral distinctions, all subside or even cancel one another out. The *Bhagavad Gita*—The Song of God—the great religious text which is among the finest and most popular sacred texts of Hinduism, also speaks of the conflicts that agitate the soul of man, of doubt, suffering and the need for consolation. In the *Bhagavad Gita*, too, reassurance lies in the divine teaching of the illusoriness of existence. Life and death do not exist, or perhaps overlap—the only truth is in the vast, eternal flow that everything bears within itself, where dying and not dying, killing and not killing, are equivalent. Hesse did not take these teachings literally, nor did he accept them in their entirety. He absorbed them, put them aside, knowing that he would need them one day, and used them a little at a time to construct his system of life. In 1912 he wrote a short essay on the *Bhagavad Gita*, and two years later, in September 1914, it became the subject of a poem. The huge conflict which would claim millions of lives had only just broken out and Hesse's lines are heavy with anguish—he sees:

> *Thousands suffering, dying, decomposing*
> *And I renounced war in my heart*
> *Blind God of pointless sorrows*
> *And yet, in an hour of dark solitude*
> *A memory comes to the surface.*[31]

That memory is the memory of an ancient Indian text, the *Bhagavad Gita*, in which, in a long dialogue between a deity and a warrior, the god calmly answers the moral doubts of someone who is about to take the lives of his fellow men by telling him that life and death are appearances which are equivalent. Hesse, in the wake of that memory, has the consoling thought that "there is no death that can touch what belongs to the spirit."[32]

CHINA

HESSE ADMIRED THE ASCETICS, but he himself was not ascetic by nature. The anguish that always hovered around him, sometimes coming closer and at other times moving away, like a bird of prey playing with its catch, was not only metaphysical in character. The conflicts that raged within him and kept him in a constant state of restlessness were also born out of a deep rift between his imagined world and the real world. The writings of the Indian mystics lessened these tensions, but were not enough in themselves to cure them. He needed a wisdom that was closer to life, more pragmatic and less absolute than that which he found in the sacred texts of India. "I was seeking in that Indian world something that could not be found there, a kind of wisdom which nowhere found expression in words, of which I nevertheless sensed the possibility and the existence, even the necessity."[33]

Hesse was led by his nature to analyse every idea he came across and then look for new ones. If he put a book aside, dissatisfied with its contents, it was only to pick up another. Feeling that the answers that came from Indian religious thinking were too lofty, he lowered his sights slightly and directed them further east, to China.

Once again, he was not the only one to do so.

China, like India before it, reawakened childhood memories in Hesse. In his time, his father had published a study on Lao-Tzu, comparing some aspects of his message to that of Christ. Then, a few years after the Indian fashion that had pervaded Germany at the turn of the century and before war came along to extinguish the old enthusiasms and ignite new ones, a similar fashion for all things Chinese spread through German intellectual circles. The great classic texts of Chinese thought had recently been published in German—the *Analects* of Confucius, the *Tao te ching* and the work of Chuang-Tzu in the edition edited by the sinologist Richard Wilhelm, whom Hesse greatly admired. When the war was over, there was a new orientalising wave, especially among the younger generation of intellectuals, in the wake of the disorientation and overturning of values that characterised the fertile, feverish Weimar age.

Many looked towards China not only out of a desire for exoticism and escape from the tottering civilisation of Europe, but because they aspired to a different system of solidarity and social duties which left its mark on the literature and the political theatre of the 1920s. It was not this, though, that attracted Hesse to China, nor was this the kind of answer he was seeking to his existential questions. The ills of society, he believed, were in a way the product and not the cause of the ills of the individual. The poetry and philosophy of ancient China, though, might provide a remedy for the malaise of the individual, in the first place his own. In a letter of 1921 to Romain Rolland, the great French writer a few years older than him, who, like him, was attracted to mysticism, he wrote of Lao-Tzu: "To me, he has been for many years the greatest source of wisdom and consolation that I know."[34] What attracted him to the figure of Lao-Tzu and to the *Tao te ching*, the *Book of the Way and of Virtue*, was its encouragement to confront life with spontaneity, to avoid any direct action to modify the course of things, because nature is benevolent in itself and it is pointless to try to force it. He loved the concrete, down-to-earth nature of a teaching that proposed modes of conduct rather than absolute truths. It is better to reduce one's own ambitions as much as possible and accept things as they are; better to try and be like water which, in nature, is always at the bottom—nothing is weaker than water and nothing is stronger. The weak conquers the strong; the soft defeats what resists it.

In the most ancient Chinese thought, which precedes Lao-Tzu and is at the basis of the *I Ching*, the great *Book of Changes*, the text of divination and oracles in which both Lao-Tzu and Confucius have common roots, Hesse finds a theme around which much of his life revolved—the duality and contrast between opposites: the human and the divine, social obligation and individual choice, gregariousness and solitude. As is well known, in the *I Ching* the world is seen as the result of the alternation between two different primal energies, the *yin*—which is the female, dark, concentration and repose—and the *yang*—which is the male, light, heat and activity. There is no contradiction in this duality because both elements are essential to life and their conjunction and disjunction, their 'changes', follow the rhythms and the multiplicity of things; good and evil, the just and the unjust necessarily belong to the same natural order of the universe.

If the whole of the human race had to be divided into two main types, says Hesse in an essay in which he collected some of his theological reflections, men would be divided into the rational and the religious.[35] Hesse knew that such a division is precarious because as soon as we place someone within one of these two categories, new elements emerge that modify that judgement, so that the separation of the two types is no longer clear and the fine universal order we thought we had configured falls to pieces. All the same, however ambiguous this basic distinction might be, Hesse did not hesitate to place himself among the religious. His, however, was a religion that did not correspond to a specific doctrine. Moving between different cultures, between various myths and traditions, between West and East, between one century and another, Hesse ended by formulating a conception in which different faiths and truths intersect and complement one another. Starting from the pietistic Christianity of his youth, passing through Indian, then Chinese thought, and also, many years later, at the suggestion of a cousin who was a scholar of all things Japanese, through Zen Buddhism, Hesse strove to gather together the elements common to all denominations and make of this his personal spiritual breviary. Beyond the practices, liturgies, and forms of worship, there were only a few basic principles—one of them is the unity that envelops the world, that resolves differences, that contains in itself—and therefore eradicates—the contrasts. It is the whole that is sensed even if it is not understood, the great metaphysical unity that overcomes time and cancels space, the greatest, highest and most consolatory thought that has been given to man. "In nothing else in the world do I believe so deeply, no other idea is as sacred to me as that of unity—the idea that the entire universe is a divine unity; that suffering and evil derive from the fact that we individuals no longer feel ourselves to be inseparable parts of a whole; that the ego considers itself too important."[36]

Hesse often returns to this thought in his daily struggle with the sense of abandonment and isolation which afflicts every modern man—even when solitude and emptiness beleaguer us, even when we feel that the community and family structures are crumbling and are unable to comfort us, we remember that we are not isolated and dispersed atoms, but that our existence belongs to an infinitely superior unity, to the great natural order of things.

SIDDHARTHA'S SECRET

T O ATTAIN THIS THOUGHT, to make this immense potential for serenity and happiness one's own, faith and the words of the sages are not enough. All the abstractions, all the metaphors, all the books in the world can only point the way. To make that journey, one is alone and it is within himself that each person must find the patience and courage that he needs.

Herein lies the secret and the deepest meaning of *Siddhartha*, the best-known, best-loved and most-debated of all Hesse's works. This story of slightly more than a hundred pages has been seen from Hindu, Buddhist, Taoist and Christian viewpoints. Some have seen in it the influence of Schopenhauer and Nietzsche, while it has also been interpreted from a psychoanalytical viewpoint. None of these readings is exhaustive, but each of them contains a kernel of truth.

Siddhartha has the subtitle *Indian Poem*, but Hesse himself said that it should not be taken literally—as we have already seen, in geographical terms the word 'India' had quite a flexible meaning for him. "My saint wears Indian clothes," Hesse wrote to Stefan Zweig in 1922, the year of the publication of *Siddhartha*, "but his wisdom is closer to Lao-Tzu than to Gotama."[37] Gotama is the Enlightened One, the Sublime, a figure close to the historical Buddha; Siddhartha admires him more than any other person he has met and, if he had to choose a master for himself, no one could be better. Nevertheless, he leaves him because he has decided not to have masters and not to follow any other way but his own.

Siddhartha is a novel with a circular structure. It comprises twelve chapters, like the hours of the day; like a circle, it begins and ends at the same point—on the bank of a river. It is a harmonious story in which various cultural and religious backgrounds effortlessly come together in an almost musical rhythm and at a calm, simple narrative pace. The images and figures are sensual and colourful, by contrast with the abstract transparency of the message they bear. The story of Siddhartha, from his lively and inquisitive youth to his mystical experience, from the worldly pleasures he enjoys to his chance arrival on the banks of a river, is a slow circular progression of the spirit which only in the final phase—the third and last part of the book—enters onto the way of truth. When Siddhartha meets the ferryman Vasudeva—a simple man who does not say much but who "like few people ... knew how to listen"[38]—and decides to stay and learn how to manoeuvre the boat and the other humble tasks necessary to the daily life of a ferryman, he begins the road back. Now that he has left the years of passion behind him, the moment has come to become a child again and find the way of innocence. All the characters of the story reappear one by one; each one wants to be carried to the other bank and the two ferrymen help the travellers and practise their tranquil profession, day after day.

One day Siddhartha's son appears. Siddhartha has never known him, but now loves him very much and regards him as the bearer of happiness. But the son does not want to stay and leaves him just as he, so many years ago, left his own father in order to follow his destiny. Everyone passes and the river carries away their images. Siddhartha watches the water flowing past and sees in it his life—the river is always the same, it goes towards the sea but could equally flow back upstream, there is no past and no present, each thing is the whole and every instant is eternity.

Here, at last, like a flower very slowly unfolding, there emerges in Siddhartha an awareness of what wisdom is and what the goal of his long search has been. A state of the soul, in Hesse's words, which is simply this—to learn to perceive, breathe and live the unity of the world. To feel that behind a thousand sufferings, a thousand contradictions and a thousand conflicts, immobile and a thousand times greater than them, is the infinite unity of the world, the only thing capable of giving peace.

EXERCISES OF WISDOM

T HE WAY OF SIDDHARTHA'S JOURNEY is a long one and it is not for everyone to see it all the way through to the end.

Hesse always liked to involve others in his experiences and his thoughts. This too, may have derived from his family heritage—from his father and his religious teachings, from his grandfather as a bearer of truth between distant peoples. He knew that abstract truths and theoretical statements were not enough, certainly not enough for everyone. Just as the practices of gardening—pruning, watering, digging—help to involve us in the reality of nature, so there exist practices that help us to sense the mysterious, sublime unity of the world. Hesse mentions them in his essays, in his letters, in some passages in his novels and also gives us some concrete indications as to the way to put them into practice—they are techniques which today are familiar to many, but which at that time were rarer and more mysterious. One of these is breathing. Hesse offered the following specific suggestions on this subject to one of the many readers who turned to him for advice: "Through experience, I realised that the most valid external aid to reaching a state of concentration and inner calm, is doing breathing exercises, derided in the West as mere navel-gazing. Do exercises like those done by the best physiotherapists; be careful never to force the breathing in, rather than the breathing out, it could be harmful. The important thing is that you breathe in as deeply as possible, concentrating exclusively on this function. It really is a great help. It helps us to distance ourselves from the present moment, and prepares us for calm and contemplation. If you accompany the breathing with an image, if you want to attribute a spiritual meaning, a content, to these exercises, imagine you are breathing not air, but Brahma, imagine you are letting the Divine enter you with every breath and then letting it out."[39]

Even more frequent in Hesse's work are references to what has always been seen, in all parts of the world, as the first exercise of spiritual ascent—meditation. He praised it at some length in his essay on the *Discourses* of Buddha, and mentions it in *Demian*, *Narcissus and Goldmund* and *Siddhartha*, where the protagonist sees through it "simultaneously all the past, present and future, and then everything is good, everything is perfect, everything is Brahma."[40] In *The Glass Bead Game*, where Hesse tries to draw together the threads of his knowledge and to express it in a great and complex metaphor, he attributes a central role to meditation among the tools that man has at his disposal to perfect himself. Josef Knecht, the protagonist of the novel, goes through a long and complex training process. From the beginning, his spiritual guide, the Music Master, informs him that, of all the disciplines that await him, meditation is the most important because it helps to distance ourselves from everyday worries. "The more our task at any given time demands of us," says the Magister, "the more dependant we are on meditation as a wellspring of energy, as the ever-renewing concord of mind and soul."[41]

The fact that Hesse harps so insistently on this theme is not coincidental, nor is it a narrative ploy. Nothing is more alien to him than pure abstraction and he never forgets—since he himself feels them—the agonising questions derived from a confrontation with reality. Meditation is "a shift in the level of consciousness"[42] and, through it, emotion and reason, logical thought and intuitive thought, instead of being in conflict, are finally reconciled.

Meditation and breathing as techniques to achieve a condition of calm and serenity are an integral part of yoga—Hesse is again anticipating the use of practices which are much better known and more widespread today than they were in the first decades of the twentieth century.

Among Hesse's many reviews of works by major and minor contemporary writers, there is one of Keyserling's *Travel Diary of a Philosopher*. One of the merits of the book that he points out is that the writer has understood the importance of the practice of yoga. Perhaps simplistically but certainly effectively, he adds that Europe has "a visceral need" for yoga.[43]

While, in the most complex and in a way the most pedagogical of his books, *The Glass Bead Game*, Hesse was reasserting the liberating virtues of meditation, another authoritative voice, this time from the scientific sphere, Carl Gustav Jung, also recognised the therapeutic function of Eastern spiritual practices. In two of his essays, one on yoga and the other on meditation, the psychiatrist and founder of analytical psychology described how, in the European cultural tradition, body and spirit are in conflict, while yoga tends to put "the body in contact with the whole of the spirit",[44] and how meditation, which leads to a state which we consider regression of the consciousness, is from the Eastern viewpoint its purest and highest expression. In a short piece called *Journey to India*, Jung also observes that, in Eastern culture, moral questions do not have the importance they have in ours—good and evil belong to nature and are nothing other, in reality, than two different aspects of the same thing.

This is a reflection which could easily have come from the pen of Hesse—hardly surprising when we remember that not only did Hesse know Jung, but also had a number of sessions of analysis with him. We have no way of knowing if the two of them ever talked about these subjects between themselves. It is likely that they were both moving in the same direction along different paths—one, rationally, in order to find a cure for the ills that afflict the individual psyche, the other, intuitively and poetically, in a spiritual journey in search of wisdom and happiness.

EVERYDAY
ENLIGHTENMENT

LOVE

THE JOURNEY THAT BROUGHT Hermann Hesse close to the source of that rare stream that we call happiness was long and, as we have seen, touched on many fields of knowledge. But, to truly reach the goal, knowledge is not enough, nor is reading, or breathing techniques, or meditation, or yoga. What a person knows, what he has learnt from books and from experience, allows him to reach the threshold of harmony and balance but in order to achieve happiness—not in an occasional and fleeting, but a stable and permanent way—there is still a step to take.

This final step is, in reality, a state of mind—an openness, not towards a single person or thing, but towards all people and all things. It is, to give it its ancient and much abused name, love. Hesse says that what counts is not only what we do, but how we do it; not only what we are, but how we are. What is done must be done with love, and all life must be lived with love. Even his Siddhartha, Hesse writes in *My Belief*, a short essay on his relationship with religion, considers "love and not knowledge as the supreme value".[45] Hesse seems almost surprised by this, as if Siddhartha were not a character created by him, as if he had studied the man's feelings in order to find the required teaching.

It is not easy to attain this general, undifferentiated 'condition of love', which is similar to what mystics feel towards all manifestations of creation, however small or large, animate or inanimate. It is not easy to attain it because we live not in abstract solitude but in the everydayness of life. And it is not easy because it is sometimes through suffering that we reach love, and, through love, the gates of happiness.

This is what happens to Siddhartha. His encounter with his son, the most unexpected and desired of all the travellers who have come to the banks of the river, makes Siddhartha hope, now that he has attained wisdom, that he will finally have someone to love. His son, though, refuses. The father tries to teach him the ways of knowledge, but is unable to teach him anything, and tries to make him stay but fails. At that moment Siddhartha feels a great sorrow, perhaps the greatest of his life. Then he realises that wisdom lies in forgiveness, and happiness in loving even those who harm us, and his outlook changes. Previously he has looked down on the 'childlike people' whose main concern is to gain power and wealth. Now he feels that they, too, are worthy of love, with all their weakness and their pathetic striving.

In the final pages of the story, Siddhartha meets again Govinda, the friend of his youth from whom he had been separated when the latter had chosen to follow the Buddha, and talks with him. "And here is a doctrine at which you will laugh. It seems to me, Govinda, that love is the most important thing in the world. It may be important to great thinkers to examine the world, to explain and despise it. But I think it is only important to love the world, not to despise it, not for us to hate each other, but to be able to regard the world and ourselves and all beings with love, admiration and respect."[46]

Like Siddhartha, Hesse had been hurt and had hurt others in his family relationships. In a year of profound crisis, when his wife Mia had started on the road to mental illness and he had been unable to help her, Hesse had written some pages in which he recognised his mistakes and the importance of a love he had not given. They are contained in a novel written in the first person, entitled *From the Diary of Martin*, which remained in a fragmentary state. "Happy is he who knows how to love,"[47] writes Hesse, and it is a theme to which he returned more or less consciously throughout his life—that love is the condition necessary for happiness; that loving is more important and necessary than being loved.

In all Hesse's works, there is not one that could really be called a love story. Love is rarely a protagonist in his novels and stories. His women are not particularly memorable—often, their description is limited to a few adjectives. What counts, for Hesse, is more the subject than the object of love; more what love produces in the person who loves than the quality of being loved.

Persuading one's fellow men that the secret of a happy life lies in loving everything around us, even humble, insignificant things, and convincingly relating such truths, which have already been said many times throughout the ages and in every language, is no easy task.

Hesse tries to do so with a deliberate simplicity, stripping his words of all metaphysical connotations. Here, too, his assertions have been confirmed by scientific research conducted long after his death by certain schools of contemporary psychology, which maintained that many acts of altruism, compassion and generosity—acts which we may, therefore, call gestures of love—produce in the people who perform them states of satisfaction and inner serenity superior to those produced by activities which we consider in themselves pleasurable and satisfying, like the company of friends, or attending a party or a show. The exhortation to love one's neighbour, so explicit in the New Testament—"Love thy neighbour as thyself"—does not, in other words, have only a moral value, does not only correspond to a divine commandment, but also meets a personal, very human desire for happiness. Hesse tells us that understanding this and accepting it on an active level demands a certain level of maturity.

In that unusual diary of thoughts entitled *A Guest at the Spa*, written a few years after *Siddhartha*, the author wonders if it is not a mistake to attempt simplistically to spread such truths, almost as if they were merchandise; if it is not a mistake, in other words, that the great repositories of wisdom, like the Gospels, can be bought in every shop or acquired for free in every church, and if it would not better to have to fight and struggle and sacrifice some of one's time, some of one's life, to become acquainted with them. This was certainly the case for Hesse, even though he had the Gospels available to him from his childhood.

In the last pages of *A Guest at the Spa*, Hesse reflects on the words "Love thy neighbour as thyself" and leads the reader to an extraordinary and unexpected revelation, which is that the phrase should be read "Love thy neighbour, because he is thyself"—not merely as a commandment but as an achievement, almost a Christian version of the Sanskrit *tat tvam asi* (that art thou).[48] This, he says, is one of the wisest things that have ever been said.

On the path towards love, we may begin with the love of small things. We have already spoken of the love of nature—bending over a tuft of grass, picking a flower, looking at a tree caressed by the wind. Nature is easy to love, because it easily returns our love. But even the most insignificant things are worthy of love. All that matters is not to be in a hurry, to have patience and look carefully, to observe the infinite variations of reality. The smallest pleasures, he says, are so scattered in everyday life, that people who lead a busy working life do not know of them or appreciate them. Their senses do not perceive what is small and does not cost anything. If anything, the poor might appreciate them a little more, but even the poor do not know that in reality the things that give the most joy are those that do not cost anything.

Bigger pleasures should be reserved perhaps for special moments, such as feast days. In these words of Hesse's, we hear the echo of a very ancient vision—life as a succession of humble everyday tasks, which from time to time bring us pain or joy, interspersed with rare celebrations.

THE ART OF LOOKING

HESSE, IN FACT, does not deny that on the way to love and joy, along with little things, there are also greater things—among them, art. The enjoyment of works of art is today within everyone's reach—it is not necessary to belong to an elite. Visits to museums and major exhibitions are one of the most common hobbies and we often see long queues in front of the ticket office for a good exhibition that has been heavily publicised in the media or for a concert by a famous conductor. Such things are considered moments of cultural enrichment, pleasure or escape. Hesse did not like fashionable cultural events and might have been surprised to see the function which art has taken on in the consumer society. Personally, apart from literature, he was much drawn to painting and music.

He tried to find in painting and music what he also found in nature, in books and in Eastern cultures—a point of support, a refuge, an aid to living. His concept of art was classical and humanist. He had a preference for a serene, Apollonian art that resolves conflicts, rather than a Dionysian art of intoxication or turmoil.

He loved words. There is no doubt that literature was the great love of his life, because in words, above all in his poetic works, he found "clarity, comfort, justification and new joy, new innocence and new love of life."[49] Consistent with his own principles, he also loved other people's words as much as his own. But painting, too, had a special place among Hesse's loves. In his youth his Italian excursions were an immersion in painting. He spent whole days at the Uffizi, visited churches, studied altarpieces, and in the pages of his diary he made

103

insightful comments on the works of the old masters, from Botticelli to Perugino.

In Venice, he enthused over Titian, Bellini, Giorgione and Veronese. Looking at old master paintings, or admiring a splendid cathedral or a nobleman's palace, he found comfort in the thought that the efforts of so many men over the centuries had not been in vain; that something important and universally valid connected them and that this gave confidence and hope to everyone. In art, as in religion, he was searching for the echo of a long-ago primal wisdom: "Every true poet has a spark of this wisdom; without it, art and religion are not possible."[50] This, for Hesse, is the huge attraction that art, whether literature, painting or music, has for man—it unites what is divided, combines the real and the spiritual, the subject and the object, and in this unity the breath of the divine can be felt.

THE ART OF PAINTING

As well as being a poet and a novelist, Hesse was a painter. And to his painting, especially in recent years, the public has unexpectedly turned, because it reveals, just as much as his words, part of his inner journey in search of balance and serenity. As in his writing, so in his painting Hesse was not afraid of repeating himself. His subjects were always the same—hills, houses, trees, lakes, flowers and clouds. Hesse was like those Byzantine painters of icons who painted an infinite number of times the same image of Mary, with tiny variations in the face, the eyes, the hand supporting the child, because in that tireless repetition of the subject and its infinite, almost imperceptible variations, the oneness and the multiplicity of the world were reflected. In the same way, the Buddhist monk repeats the same mantra ad infinitum and, in doing so, finds peace. In Hesse's paintings, there are no human figures and no trace of movement—nature is immobile, the houses are uninhabited or their inhabitants absent, and there are no animals in the gardens. The combinations of colours vary—vibrant reds or bright yellows, electric blues on the serene background of the hills of Canton Ticino. Hesse's watercolours were intended as a personal exercise, rather than to be admired by others. Their reason for being lay in the very act of painting. They were, in reality, a structured, durable therapy, a means of attaining inner harmony, and that harmony is reflected in those who contemplate them. This, perhaps, together with Hesse's fame, is one of the secrets of their success. That this was indeed the case, that painting represented one of the things that helped him to put order in his thoughts—and not coincidentally, but with the encouragement of his analyst—Hesse admitted explicitly in a letter to a writer friend: "It is a fact that I would have been dead long ago if, in the darkest moment of my existence, I had not found consolation and salvation in my first attempts at painting."[51]

THE ART OF LISTENING

Music, TOO, had an important consolatory function for Hesse. When he was very young, he had learnt the violin. Intellectually, he placed music on the highest level of the human mind's ability to get close to the divine. In music, more clearly than in any other art form, there is that *goldene Spur*, that golden trace which is none other than the very imprint of divinity.

If Hesse's love of painting was born during his early manhood, his love of music goes much further back. It was in fact an integral part of the family's culture, as was not uncommon in German families at the time. Hesse once wrote to his sister Adele that without music—both music played within the family and in church—his childhood would not have been the same. Even though Hesse's human and artistic personality can, in many ways, be related to the turbulent universe of Romanticism, his musical tastes went in quite another direction, towards the great baroque and classical masters, from Bach and Händel to Gluck and above all Mozart, who represented a kind of end point. Bach was the ultimate sublimation of Christian order, reason elevated to the level of God, but Mozart was perfection achieved, light-heartedness, divine joy. Mozart, like Goethe, belonged to the kingdom of the Immortals.

Like all the stages in Hesse's path towards love and happiness, music, too, had an important place in his literary work. In *Steppenwolf*, the most tormented and doubt-filled of his novels, the protagonist/Hesse is dismayed to discover, through a music he has never heard before (when the book was written, jazz had just arrived in Europe with the first 78 rpm records), the existence of an entire unknown world in which the traditional

107

values of morality and behaviour have been overturned. The book ends with a solemn and enigmatic phrase that symbolises the future destiny of his character and of himself: "Mozart was waiting for me."[52]

The role of music is even more prominent and crucial in *The Glass Bead Game*, where the whole of the hypothetical society imagined by Hesse at its highest level is constructed on a mathematical-musical system—music is play, it is art, it is the architecture on which the perfect model for man's life is based.

LIVING WITH THE FLOW OF TIME

E VERYTHING, THEN, is worthy of love—small things and great art; the humblest, most modest moments and the great events of life; the important figures who cross our paths and the small everyday encounters. Even our fragile bodies should be loved, not more than all other things, but like all other things. Old age too, even old age, should be loved. In a world that worships youth and beauty, that may appear an eccentric statement. This was not the case in other periods, nor is it the case, even today, in other cultures—the East still venerates the old in a way that may seem paradoxical to us. Hesse does not assert that old age is superior, although he is well aware that he would not have completed his inner journey without the passing of the years. Old age and youth are equivalent: "Maturity," he says, "is not worse than youth, Lao-Tzu is not worse than Buddha. Blue is not worse than red."[53]

For old age to have a meaning (and how could it not have one, since it is part of nature, a journey that every being in creation undertakes?) it is necessary, Hesse explains, to say yes. An old man is ridiculous if he thinks he is young, and a young person thinking he is more mature than he is, is equally ridiculous. Both are deluding themselves that they can transgress the natural order of things. Even the garden of old age has its flowers—its colours are less bright, perhaps, but no less attractive. In the garden of old age, the flower of patience, for example, blooms wonderfully, as does its twin, the flower of forgiveness. And, if it is really a garden and not a wild no man's land, it is dominated by the plant of acceptance, of 'saying yes'. The years of late maturity, and then those of old age, were to be the most serene of Hesse's life. His intellectual progress and his family relationships had been shaken by storms, contradictions and struggles; he had been afflicted by recurrent physical ailments and, at the same time, filled with a frantic desire to overcome all the ills of the world with his mind. On the day of his fiftieth birthday he had written a poem in which he had cursed his age for depriving him of the joy of hugging a beautiful curly-haired girl—all he could do now was read Goethe. More than once, as a young man and as an adult, he had thought of taking his own life. Of all the seasons, the one that most troubled him, because of the impulses and stirrings it aroused, was spring. But as he continued on his long road to wisdom, as he discovered the miraculous virtue of love, Hesse realised that old age, with the fading of the life force and the charitable selection that memory makes of the past, brought sweetness.

Not even death caused fear, because it, too, is an extreme part of life. Every moment in life has its flowering, and every season is followed by a new one in a journey with numberless steps. A poem by Hesse entitled *Stages* ends like this:

> *Even the hour of our death may send*
> *Us speeding on to fresh and newer spaces,*
> *And life may summon us to newer races.*
> *So be it, heart: bid farewell without end.*[54]

THE THOUSAND TALENTS
OF RABINDRANATH TAGORE

THE LORD OF THE SUN

IF WE WERE TO DEFINE HESSE BY HIS LIFE, and judge him by his fears and anxieties, it would be difficult to speak of him as a guide to harmony and wisdom, let alone a teacher of happiness. For reasons that in a way are the opposite, it would be equally hard to attach such a definition to Tagore. Hesse had a long, tormented life, which only grew calmer in his last years; Tagore led a prestigious, frenetic life, which, like Hesse's, only found a degree of tranquillity towards the end. Both of them, the former through his faults, the latter through excess, struggled in life to achieve the harmony and moderation they taught others.

Almost from birth, and in some respects from even before it, Rabindranath Tagore seemed predestined for fame—because of his family, his wealth, his good looks, his intelligence, the extraordinary curiosity of his mind and his astonishing energy. He was a poet, a musician, a playwright, a novelist, a painter, a pedagogue, a thinker and a farmer. It was with some justification that Albert Schweitzer, the no less versatile philanthropist, doctor and thinker, called Tagore "an Indian Goethe". His destiny was even written in his name—*Rabi* is a Bengali word derived from the Sanskrit *ravi*, meaning 'sun'. Rabindranath can be read as 'lord of the sun'. We have hundreds of images of him, at every age, in every pose and in the company of the most diverse people, from members of his family to world leaders, kings and scientists, artists and politicians, all of whom got on well with a 'lord of the sun' who, like the sun, went from East to West and then back to the East, and so on. When he was young, he had large dark eyes and an intense gaze, a haughty bearing and clothes to match; then, as he grew older, with his long

113

white hair, flowing beard, and loose-fitting full-length tunics, an arcane omnipotence seemed to emanate from him.

How is it possible, we may ask, that this proud, versatile man, who was at his ease with heads of state and government, was also able to interpret the secret desires of people less fortunate than himself in such a way that they regarded him as their guide? That in the West he was seen as the highest expression of the East and in the East as a man who bridged both worlds, and that his message was so simple, humble almost, and intelligible to everyone?

Tagore was, in fact, a dazzling, enigmatic figure, an enlightened but profoundly contradictory mind. One of his most authoritative biographers, Krishna Kripalani, who knew him well when he was alive and married his granddaughter, has recalled that once, when Tagore was already well advanced in years and laden with honours and celebrity, he was asked what he considered his best quality. Tagore replied, "Inconsistency." When asked what was his greatest failing, he replied, "The same."[55]

AN EXAMPLE OF INCONSISTENCY

WHETHER A QUALITY or fault, inconsistency was one of the dominant characteristics of Tagore's multifaceted life. Another was restlessness—a physical restlessness, before anything else, which drove him to travel constantly, to change residences and ways of life. Even when age and ill health restricted his movements, he continued to move from one to another of his houses at Santiniketan. An intellectual restlessness, too, which drove him to tackle every literary genre and, in the field of poetry—in which his achievement was most notable and to which his name is most often linked—to attempt every style, from the traditional to the new and experimental. With inexhaustible curiosity, he also tried his hand at other arts—at music and singing as a young man, and then, at the age of almost seventy, at painting—and not a calm style of painting that followed classical rules, but, rather, a furious expression of inner turmoil. Behind the serene appearance of someone who judges the ills of the world and his own ills from on high, behind the composed figure of an enlightened aristocrat who invariably discharged the duties that his social position and the morality of his country demanded, was a man torn by contradictory impulses and inner conflicts. "I sometimes detect within myself," he wrote in a letter, "a battleground where two opposing forces are constantly in action, one beckoning me to peace and cessation of all strife, the other egging me on to battle. It is as though the restless energy and the will to action of the West were perpetually assaulting the citadel of my Indian placidity."[56]

In this he resembled Hesse, who was also perpetually torn between highs and lows, between opposing impulses, temptations and thoughts. Like Hesse, Tagore, in order to defend himself from forces driving him in different directions and to escape from the burden of too much talent, too much imagination, found solace in the reassuring idea of a primal stability, an overarching unity in which everything can find order. This is the basic element in Rabindranath Tagore's conception of life—the free development of the human personality in every direction, the certainty that there is no real contradiction between demands which we consider opposites, such as flesh and spirit, nature and the divine being, the love of life and the love of God, the aspiration to beauty and the temptation of vanity, the demands of society and the rights of individuals, loyalty to traditions and the acceptance of the new, love for one's own people and love of mankind in general.

It is startling how close Tagore was to a modern sensibility, to the notion, so widespread today (of which globalisation itself is, if we wish, a corollary), that life is not based on a scale of hierarchically ordered values and that all values, even when they contradict one another, are encompassed within an immanent natural unity. Starting from that point, Tagore, like Hesse, strove to look not for what divides West and East but for what unites them, not what distinguishes the different religions but what is common to all of them. Or even, a level closer to the individual sensibility, to enjoy what the world has to offer without becoming its slave, or to confront suffering and accept it for what it is—not an absolute but a 'fragment' of the whole.

A VAST OUTPUT

THESE PRINCIPLES HOLD TOGETHER a life that, on the surface, appears quite chaotic—pulled in an infinite number of directions. We find echoes of them in his poetry, essays and letters, and in the lectures he gave in the most disparate circumstances and on the most varied subjects, but which can all be reduced to a few basic themes. Tracing Tagore's ideas in his writings is no easy task—excessive in everything, he produced a vast output, which can barely be contained in almost thirty volumes. In such a mass of work, there is, as can easily be imagined, a great deal of unevenness—some of it is good, some is very good, and there is some that is mediocre. Along with all the many honours he received during his life, of which the Nobel Prize was the most illustrious and politically significant, there were also reservations and more critical judgements. Some intellectuals who originally hailed the appearance on the Western cultural scene of this man of letters from India as a breath of fresh air, subsequently retreated. For example, W B Yeats, who was the first to give Tagore the kind of reception that is given to great men, writing a highly flattering preface to the English translation of *Gitanjali*, modified his judgement some years later. Certainly, when Tagore assumed the mantle of a public figure, indeed a political figure, many people, especially in the English-speaking world, were dismayed, especially as his involvement in public life was partly in the context of opposition to British colonial domination. The many contradictions that, as we have seen, characterised his behaviour can be evaluated differently if related to the inspiration of a poet or the positions of a public man. He was, to give one example, a passionate defender of the role of women and of female emancipation, but arranged his daughter's marriages, the first at the age of fourteen and the second when she was not yet twelve.

Nevertheless, despite changing opinions and different sensitivities, Tagore remains without doubt one of the most significant figures in twentieth-century literature and one of the most unusual and charismatic personalities ever to have travelled the five continents. In his country of origin he is still considered a major figure, almost the equal of Gandhi, not only because of what he said and wrote, but also because of what he did, the fields that he cultivated, the improvements he introduced and the institutions he created. In Europe, his fame is perhaps less universal and his popularity less ostentatious, but there are still a number of institutions that carry his name—the Tagore Society in Britain, the Tagore Centre at Villaverla in Italy, a prestigious prize named after him in Germany, to name but a few—as indeed often happens to those who, along with a literary and artistic heritage, leave men a lesson in spirituality and peace.

FAMILY TRADITIONS

A HUGE FAMILY, a rich and influential grandfather with a life-style so opulent it could be called princely, a strict father with an intense spiritual life, a mother in whose salon writers and artists gathered, fourteen children of whom Rabindranath was the youngest. From the imposing house at Jorasanko in Calcutta, the Tagores played a major role in the political, religious and cultural life of Bengal. At the time of Rabindranath's birth, India was on the verge of a period of institutional change and social upheaval, which would end with independence a few years after his death in 1941. From the East India Company, which had more or less controlled the country since the eighteenth century, although under the increasing vigilance of the British Parliament, sovereignty had passed to the crown. Then, in 1876, Benjamin Disraeli proclaimed Queen Victoria Empress of India—a territory that comprised not only today's India but also Pakistan in the West and Bangladesh in the East. It was now that the English language, educational system and administrative structures took permanent root in the Indian subcontinent, marking its life for ever and generating in the population, especially in its upper echelons, those ambivalent feelings of admiration and rejection commonly felt by the dominated towards their dominators. Calcutta was the capital of the empire and, with Bengal, its economic and intellectual centre. Here a number of cultural and religious movements were created which challenged tradition. One such was the Brahmo-Samaj—of which Debendranath, the father of Tagore, was a leading light—which aimed to reform Hinduism by absorbing principles from other great religions of the world, emphasising its deeper meaning while rejecting cruel practices such as suttee, the immolation of widows on their husbands' funeral pyres, and promoting a return to the ancient sacred scriptures of the Vedas and the Upanishads.

Tagore wrote that the unconventional conduct of his family was a result of the mixture of three cultures—the Hindu, the Muslim and the English. Referring later to the transformations of society at the time of his father and his grandfather he observed with wonderful cogency that this was the period when the loose clothes, courtly manners and generosity of the idle classes of India all fell under the axe, to be replaced by Victorian customs.[57]

Rabindranath's mother was an open-minded woman of marked artistic interests. In her house, artists and thinkers met, Goethe was read in German, Maupassant in French and Kalidasa's drama *Sakuntala* in Sanskrit; poetry was recited and the latest articles in the Bengali cultural reviews were discussed. In this cultured environment, Rabindranath began writing verse early. His mother died when he was barely thirteen, leaving him with a sense of solitude that the rare and occasional presence of his stern father did not in any way alleviate. Young Tagore spent much of his childhood and adolescence in the solitary confines of a huge house, under the strict supervision of the servants, listlessly dreaming of the outside world and the freedom of nature.

School, instead of being an alternative, was a torment. Like Hesse, Rabindranath hated school, from the moment he set foot in it until, at the age of fourteen, he abandoned it altogether. What he hated was not studying but the tediously repetitious methods with which studying was imposed; not the practice of learning, but the teachers to whom learning was entrusted.

When he was seventeen, his father decided that the young man should continue his education in England.

Young Tagore knew England through literature, theatre and poetry, but had no idea of the reality. He imagined a small island—not an inaccurate judgement, compared with the

120

vastness of India—where the inhabitants recited Tennyson or read Byron from morning to night. As it turned out, his stay of almost two years was a positive experience. Tagore, as can be imagined, experienced moments of homesickness and solitude in the grey London winters, but also happy days. It was at this time that, thanks to the good relations he established with his host family in London, he began to lay the foundation of the idealistic construction to which he remained faithful for the rest of his life—that there are no barriers between East and West that cannot be crossed and that the values and aspirations of men are the same in whatever part of the world they were born or live. Between the mind of Mrs Scott, wife of Doctor Scott, master of the house in Bloomsbury where Rabindranath lived, and the mind of a gentle Indian wife there was, in Tagore's eyes, no substantial difference.[58]

By the time he returned to Calcutta, Tagore was a cultured, handsome, impeccably dressed young man with an undeniable literary vocation. He improvised poems, and wrote essays and plays—a collection of poems entitled *Sandhya Sangit* (*Songs of the Evening*), earned him the title of the 'Shelley of Bengal' because of the strongly romantic sensibility it displayed.

That was perfectly natural for a young man of his age, in those years and with that particular cultural baggage. But something genuinely romantic now entered his life, something that he himself and his biographers subsequently shrouded in mystery and silence. Tagore had gone to live with one of his brothers, Jyotirindranath, and his sister-in-law Kadambari, first in the French settlement of Chandernagore and then in Calcutta. Kadambari, as we can see from photographs of the time, was young, slim and frail. We also know that she was cultured and sensitive. That some kind of feelings developed between Rabindranath and his beautiful sister-in-law was almost inevitable. How far they went, however, there is no way of knowing. What we do know is that, not long afterwards, Rabindranath married the very young daughter of one of his father's clerks and, the following year, Kadambari took her own life. The image of Kadambari was to remain with him for the rest of his life, even appearing in works written when he was an old man. His marriage, on the other hand, was, if not passionate, certainly successful. Mrinalini Devi was only ten when they married, she was neither cultured nor beautiful, but she was a loyal, understanding person, who brought five children into the world and gave the restless Rabindranath the help and support he needed. It should be said, incidentally, that in the strict Indian caste system, the Tagore family's marriages were usually at a lower level than their high rank would have demanded. The rumour—which may only have been envy and gossip—was that the ritual purity of the family had been tarnished in a previous generation by the actions of a Muslim who had intentionally involved a Tagore in a sacrilegious and humiliating situation.

THE DISCOVERY OF RURAL INDIA

AT THAT TIME, Rabindranath was consumed with a passion for seeing, knowing and understanding the things of the world and for expressing them in words. His father, seeing him in this dreamy state, tried to bring him back to reality by entrusting him with the task of being the *zamindar*, or administrator, of a vast family property. Some years passed, however, before he actually took up this role. Instead, he began once again to travel, leaving his child wife in India, in a furious impatience—his own words—and in a frenzied search for his own identity. With every journey, he spilled out essays and plays inspired by Western literature—Dante and Beatrice, Petrarch and Laura, Goethe and his loves—but also a first, mature collection of poetry, *Manasi* (*The Lady of the Mind*).

He was already thirty when he took possession of the lands on the banks of the River Padma in East Bengal that his father had entrusted to him. It was a moment of his intellectual development that would leave a deep mark on him. This was the first time he had come into contact with the rural world, with the work of the peasants, and with poverty and disease. On a boat, he sailed along the river and observed the lives of the humble villagers on its banks—the children bathing, the girls walking with jars on their hips, their saris swaying, entered his imagination and became characters in his works. This was also the time in which he gradually assumed a public persona, both through the recognition he received in the literary field—his output of poetry and stories was unstoppable and he was soon considered one of the greatest Bengali writers—and through his first cautious steps onto the local political scene, which met with increasing success.

These were the beginnings of restless times for India. The British gave the Hindus and Muslims the option of choosing separate representatives, which ended up exacerbating, rather than soothing, religious tensions, especially in Bengal where the population was divided, east and west, into two huge religious blocs.

SANTINIKETAN—THE REALISATION OF A UTOPIA

I F RABINDRANATH'S FATHER had thought that by putting him in charge of such a substantial property he would encourage good business sense in his son, he had made a big mistake. Tagore left East Bengal after about ten years and chose instead to settle in Santiniketan, a family possession where, some time earlier, his father had founded an ashram, a place of prayer and meditation. It was a dry, flat area of red earth, as devoid of vegetation as it was empty of people. Here he thought of combining the two things he felt most strongly—his love for things of the spirit, for poetry and words, and the social and humanitarian impulse that his direct experience of the lives of humble people tied to the land had aroused in him. It was here, a hundred and fifty kilometres north of Calcutta, and a few kilometres from Bolpur, in a remote place, which at the time could only be reached by ox cart, that Tagore settled, founding first a school and then an international university, which was to become one of the most famous and innovative in the whole continent. And it was here that he began to think about ways to help men to be happier. It was a vague, generalised intuition, which he had not yet formulated explicitly, but the school he founded was a first step towards realising it.

His own school years had left him, as we have seen, with unpleasant memories. Tagore wanted a different kind of school, a free school, which would teach contact with nature and encourage a natural development of the personality. In this concept are echoes of ancient Indian ideals together with traces of innovative educational ideas that were emerging at the time in Europe and would come to fruition some time later in the experiments of Maria Montessori and Rudolf Steiner. It was essential to Tagore that the school be open to every caste and every religious denomination, that besides the traditional subjects—mathematics, Sanskrit and English—the Bengali language should also be taught, along with manual activities such as weaving, ceramics or gardening, and that time should be set aside for cultural activities like singing and dancing. Education was not an end in itself but a means to an end, and it was impossible to use the same formula for everyone indiscriminately—every man and every woman should be given the appropriate tools with which to learn the values of morality and art and freely choose their own path.

Among the first pupils to attend the school were Rabindranath's eldest son, a friend of his and some boys from the area. Teachers and pupils lived together. It was a simple, almost ascetic life, but despite this—or perhaps because of this—a serene, happy one. On Tagore's part, the foundation of the school was a noble gesture, but it could hardly be called profitable. He ploughed so much of his inheritance into it that his wife was forced to sell her jewellery in order to help her husband. But the school continued to absorb the family's financial resources, including the income from Rabindranath's books and literary prizes. It was a constant commitment, and the one still point in a multifaceted and even disorganised life. It was at Santiniketan that Tagore's true spiritual and intellectual personality emerged, and the image was established of a master of life and thought, a preacher of tolerance and harmony, which stayed with him until his death. It was this tolerance, this harmony that he saw as the path to happiness, and he did not limit himself to suggesting it in words, but also put it into practice, however imperfectly, in his teaching. His essays on the subject, and the public lectures he gave at Santiniketan, give a clear idea of how the words 'education' and 'happiness' can, in Tagore's vision, be harmonised.

Meanwhile, the situation in India and Bengal was worsening. The first years of the twentieth century coincided with the decision of the recently appointed Viceroy of India, Lord Curzon, to split Bengal administratively into two distinct entities, one, in the west, predominantly Hindu, and the other, in the east, with a Muslim majority. It was a difficult decision, and undoubtedly a farsighted one, given what religious conflict has done to the continent of Asia throughout the century and beyond, but it was an act which, at the time, was seen by the Indian people generally as an abuse of power and by the Bengalis as an attack on the integrity of the region. The reaction was immediate and certainly more violent than Lord Curzon had expected. A *svadesi*—a boycott of foreign goods—was proclaimed, which became the symbol of the struggle for Bengali self-government and then, in various forms, for the independence of India.

This was the real beginning of Tagore's involvement in Bengali politics. He was now a *gurudev*, a venerable master, at the height of his powers, considered not only a great poet but also an authentic interpreter of his country's culture. The supporters of the boycott asked him to deliver speeches at their meetings and to write verses for their songs. Tagore agreed, even though his own convictions made him lean more towards a moderate position, rejecting violence as a form of political struggle as well as any kind of narrow nationalism or sectarianism. These were, therefore, years that were full of contradictions and questions on both a political and a moral level. But, above all, they were tragic years for Tagore personally.

In 1902, soon after Tagore settled in Santiniketan, Mrinalini Devi, the wife he had married when she was still a child and who was not yet thirty, fell ill with an unidentified disease and died after a few months. In the meantime, his second daughter, Renuka, had contracted tuberculosis. The doctors suggested a rest cure in the Himalayas, and Rabindranath accompanied her there. But the change of climate did not help, and Renuka died in the autumn of 1903. The following year he lost one of his closest colleagues at Santiniketan, a talented young poet of whom Rabindranath was very fond. In 1905 his father died and, two years later, his eleven-year-old son was struck down by cholera. Four young lives had been snuffed out in the space of five years, and his family circle had been irreparably shattered. His three remaining children lived far way. Tagore was alone, and would remain alone for the rest of his life.

This was a dark, difficult period for him, filled with bouts of sadness and depression. Tagore overcame it with great strength of mind, bravely pursuing the project to which he had devoted himself in accordance with his notion of man's destiny. The poems he wrote during those years reflect his state of mind—they seem to be searching for a dialogue with the dead, and many are addressed to, or evoke, the figures of children.

In this calm acceptance of grief, in this ability to reassemble the fragments of existence into a single great unity, lies the essence of Tagore's teaching. The idea that death and life are not in conflict, but live together in the mind and fate of man, was not new to him but was one of his deepest beliefs.

TOWARDS THE NOBEL PRIZE

T HIS TIME OF MISFORTUNE gave rise to one of the most intense phases of Tagore's whole life, as regards both the development of his ideas, and his artistic output. "He slept very little, often only three or four hours," writes Edward J Thompson, one of the first Western scholars of his life and work. "The moonlight always called him outside … he was beside himself, he would enter into a state of ecstasy and spend the night under the trees."[59] Grief, instead of destroying him, had cast his mind upwards, in a mystical-religious transfiguration.

Those years, and the ones immediately following, saw the publication of some of his most inspired collections of poetry, including *Sisu* (*Child*) and *Smaran* (*Memory*). *Gitanjali* (*Song Offerings*) dates from 1910 and marks perhaps the height of his religious trajectory. In it, the poet expresses his gratitude to God not only for the good things he has given him, but also for the sufferings he has inflicted on him, because it is the way of sorrow that leads man to perfection.

The aspiration to the sublime did not make Tagore forget the miseries and difficulties of his time. Some of his poems, like those contained in the collection called *Naivedya* (*Offering*), combine religious themes with patriotic sentiments and, as well as essays and plays which today we would call 'politically aware', Tagore wrote *Gora*, a novel set against the background of the social and political reality of the country, the boycott and the independence struggle. But the ultimate message is not a message of war but of peace; his appeal is not to intransigence but to understanding and tolerance. Tagore had learnt to navigate the waters of political passion without being swept away or having to change course.

The years immediately before the First World War would be crucial to his public image. Tagore was no longer just an enlightened Bengali poet, he was already one of the greatest figures in Indian literature. Now all that remained was to take a great leap and make his entrance on the world cultural stage. Once again it was a journey that provided the opportunity. Tagore left for England in 1912, accompanied by his son Rathindranath and his daughter-in-law. During the journey he translated a selection of poems from his latest collections into rhythmic English prose. In London his friend, the painter William Rothenstein, who had been his guest in India some time earlier, gave the newly translated work to W B Yeats to read. Yeats was already widely considered to be one of the greatest poets in the English language, and his praise immediately opened the door to the Macmillan publishing house. The collection was published under the title *Gitanjali*, with an introduction by Yeats himself. Tagore immediately became a name to be reckoned with in one of the most important literary centres in Europe, and was welcomed in intellectual circles. Among those he met at this time were the poet Ezra Pound, the philosopher Bertrand Russell and the critic Ernest Rhys, who would later be one of his first biographers.

His was, in fact, a new and unusual voice in the literary scene of the time; a voice that placed man on a mystical path of trans-figuration and invoked peace and fraternity, while all around him hymns were being sung to military valour and factories were busy producing weapons of war. His works, wrote Yeats, came from a tradition in which "poetry and religion are the same thing" and from "a world I have dreamt of all my life long".[60]

Apart from his poetry, those who met him were struck by his appearance. With his long, greying beard, and intense, deep-set eyes, Tagore seemed like the embodiment of Eastern wisdom; a prophet who had come from afar, bearing a message of hope. His friend Rothenstein's son recalls him wearing a full-length robe of raw silk and a turban on his head. Tagore's appearance surprised and enchanted the cultured circles of Edwardian London and many admirers came just to see him sitting with his eyes focused on some vague point in the distance, seeming at the same time both present and remote.

In the autumn of the same year, 1912, Tagore was invited by Harvard University to give a series of lectures, which were then repeated in London the following spring and published under the title *Sadhana*. Tagore was a skilled and effective orator; it was no coincidence that the various Indian nationalist movements competed to have him at their congresses. The success his lectures met with in America was undoubtedly also partly due to the effectiveness of his presentation. But *Sadhana* touches on the themes that were occupying Tagore's thoughts in those years and which revolve around the great questions of man's destiny—love, the search for beauty, the meaning of work and suffering, the aspiration of every human being to live life to the full and to find the way to harmony and happiness.

Although he refused to be the spokesman for a unified philosophical system or religious creed, let alone an organised religion, the idea he expounded in *Sadhana* was that the divine can be recognised in all living things. He also warned against a danger which, he felt, hung over the West—the danger of believing that the future depended on constant progress in technology and science and that this might indeed be the ultimate meaning of existence.

In the wake of the interest aroused by *Gitanjali* and the stir caused by his university lectures, three more books by Tagore appeared in England that were to remain, like *Gitanjali*, among his best loved— the poetry collections *The Crescent Moon*, *The Gardener* and the play *Chitra*. This period spent in Europe had, in other words, turned out to be extremely fruitful. And it became even more so when Rabindranath learnt, in September, during his return journey to India, that he had been awarded the Nobel Prize for Literature. He was the first Asian writer to be recognised by the Nobel committee, and it made him, in a way, a symbol of the entire continent's culture and a source of pride for his countrymen. The same year, the University of Calcutta awarded him an honorary degree.

A SOLITARY PACIFIST

A LL TAGORE'S WORKS, his essays as well as his poems, are inspired by principles of brotherhood and peace. Apart from his talent, this, too, was surely on the minds of the Nobel committee when they chose him and made him world-famous. But history was moving in quite a different direction and, less than a year later, Europe blew apart. The outbreak of the First World War disturbed Tagore deeply—he had always asserted, alongside the value of Indian culture and spirituality, the greatness of Western civilisation. Now this vast cradle of reason and knowledge was destroying itself in a pointless and brutal war.

Instinctively, Rabindranath grew even closer to all those who opposed the culture of militarism and domination. In 1915 came his first encounter at Santiniketan with Gandhi, who stayed there for a week. This was the beginning of a long-lasting friendship based on deep mutual respect. True, they sometimes disagreed, not about principles, but about the way to assert those principles.

The voices of those who still believed in tolerance and friendship between peoples were, in those years, few and relatively weak. It was natural for those few to come together. One of them was Romain Rolland, who, as he did with Hesse, established a bond with Tagore that would last for a very long time. When the war was over, Rolland asked him to be one of the signatories of the *Declaration of the Independence of the Spirit*, a manifesto of values and principles to which various European artists and intellectuals subscribed. When, in 1915, the British government conferred a knighthood on Tagore, the more radical circles within Bengali culture were highly critical of him. Rabindranath reacted by indirectly defending his position in the novel *Ghare Baire* (*The Home and the World*), where the two terms reflect the eternal contrast between the internal and the external, the self and Bengal, India and the world. In his poetry, too, as in the collection *Balaka* (*A Flight of Swans*), secular concerns take precedence over the mystical fervour of the previous years.

Not long afterwards, he left for a lecture tour in America and Japan. Here, too, subjects dictated by contemporary reality occupied an important place. The lectures would later be published in two books—*Personality* and *Nationalism*. The latter is a challenge, elevated in tone but harsh in substance, to the idea that nations are the primary and natural objects of the loyalty of citizens and that national interests should have pre-eminence over every other individual or group interest. This was an argument designed to provoke angry reactions, as indeed it did, especially in Japan, which was then engaged in a process of military expansion in the Pacific and in Manchuria (and, twenty-five years later, in India too). Tagore returned to India in the darkest, bloodiest year of the war. Wisely, he took his eyes away from the present and made an effort to look to the future. He felt that his deepest vocation was to be moderate rather than extreme, because the way of enlightenment and knowledge was the middle way. His role, he felt, was that of a mediator, helping to identify what was fundamental and eternal in the heritage of both East and West. That was what gave him the idea of adding to the existing school at Santiniketan the much larger project of a university where both traditions would be integrated; where India would offer the best of its own culture and be enriched by that of the West.

The meeting of East and West, he wrote in a letter to a friend in 1920, is the most important question of our time. The name he chose for his university was Visva-Bharati, from the Sanskrit *visva* (world) and *bharati* (culture or knowledge)—it could be translated as 'universe of wisdom'. And universal it would be, with its multilingual library and with its teaching staff and pupils coming from many different countries. Visva-Bharati was to become the main focus for Tagore's interests and activities, and he would devote most of his time and his fortune to it. Because of the place chosen, the close connection it would always maintain with nature, the nobility of its inspiration and the richness of its realisation, it became something that rarely happens in a man's life—the ideal physical manifestation of a whole way of thinking and existing. It was not, however, easy to keep running, at least not until, after twenty years, the Indian government assumed the financial burden.

Visva-Bharati helped to train whole generations of major figures in the art, literature, politics and human sciences of the subcontinent—great directors like Satyajit Ray, who called the three years he spent at Santiniketan the most fruitful of his life; key figures in the history of modern India, like Indira Gandhi; or economists like Amartya Sen, who acknowledged his great debt to Visva-Bharati in his Nobel Prize acceptance speech.

And yet Tagore was not content. The university had only just got off the ground when he decided to set up, at Sriniketan, a centre for teaching the rural classes more rational farming techniques. The project attracted the collaboration of a group of enthusiasts—his son Rathindranath, an English agronomist named Leonard K Elmhirst, who was well known in the United States, and a rich American heiress, Dorothy Whitney Straight, without whose generosity the initiative would never have been realised. Tagore's conception was the same as that which had inspired his first school, twenty years earlier—to combine the education of the mind with a model of a simple, free, joyful life. The new centre would teach not only the principles of balanced and economically sound farming, but also the techniques of local craftsmen, as well as folk songs and dances. It was important for everyone—peasants, students and teachers—to share both an educational experience and the wider, more joyful aspects of rural life.

With the end of the war—during which India had made a major contribution to the British victory and suffered many casualties—the movement of civil disobedience against British domination resumed. The inspiration came above all from Gandhi, and it was Tagore who gave him the name Mahatma—great soul—which was to remain with him. The Empire reacted by declaring martial law in the most insubordinate regions. In Amritsar, a city in the Punjab where Tagore, at the age of twelve, had written his first poem while travelling with his father, the troops commanded by General Dyer responded to a demonstration by opening fire, killing almost four hundred. Tagore joined in the general indignation, going so far as to return the knighthood he had received three years earlier to the Viceroy of India, Lord Chelmsford. But his support of the independence movement, and especially the boycott of foreign goods—a boycott symbolised by the spinning wheel, which became a fixture in Indian homes—was lukewarm and contradictory. Tagore found Gandhi's calls to boycott foreign textiles reminiscent of an outdated nationalism, and the great bonfire of those textiles, timed to coincide with the arrival of the Prince of Wales, seemed to him an unfortunate rhetorical gesture. He expounded these ideas in a lecture he gave in Calcutta,[61] to which Gandhi responded skilfully with an article in which he called Tagore "the great sentinel" who warns everyone against the excesses of bigotry and intolerance. He subsequently tried to win Tagore back to his cause, paying him a visit in Calcutta and attempting to persuade him to resume his place in the movement for civil disobedience. The attempt failed and Tagore distanced himself even more from the political scene. This did not end his friendship with Gandhi—many years later, when the Mahatma was incarcerated by the British and had begun a hunger strike in support of the untouchables, Tagore went to see him and, taking advantage of his name and prestige, suggested a compromise solution, which was accepted. Subsequently, Gandhi gradually relinquished the responsibilities of active politics, leaving Jawaharlal Nehru to lead Congress.

A TIRELESS TRAVELLER

A S TAGORE'S DETACHMENT from internal Indian affairs became more marked, his curiosity and his permanent restlessness, the pressing invitations he received from around the world and the need to raise funds for his various educational projects drove him increasingly to travel. For about fifteen years, between 1916 and 1932, he was almost always on the move. Some of his journeys lasted a few months, others more than a year. He again visited England, then France, Germany, Italy, Belgium, Austria, Switzerland, the Scandinavian countries and the Balkans. He visited Japan twice, China and the whole of South-East Asia, Latin America, Egypt, Iran and Iraq, the United States on many occasions and, once, the Soviet Union.

In Tagore, every gesture, every act of everyday life takes place on two levels—one is factual, concrete, and has its beginning and end in a rational need; the other is intimate and transfigured and results in poetry. His journeys and lectures may well have been inspired above all by the need to replenish the financial resources absorbed by so many ambitious and costly projects, and were certainly, at times, accompanied by understandable surges of vanity, but the impulse to change scenery and explore the unknown belonged to his deepest nature. "You may have read in books," Tagore wrote to a young woman in 1918, when this frenetic restlessness of his was again beginning to manifest itself, "that some birds leave their nests at certain times and fly away over the sea. I am such a bird."[62] The collection containing some of the most elevated and beautiful poems that Tagore ever wrote, entitled *Balaka* (as so often a difficult word to translate, suggesting a flock of birds passing in the sky) is inspired by the idea of an irresistible urge to migrate, the sense of a calling that distances us from the places we know and draws us to those we do not. "For the time is over—the time of waiting in the port," he repeats several times in one of these poems. And the final lines of another poem are:

> *I hear the countless voices of the human heart*
> *Flying unseen,*
> *From the dim past to the dim unblossomed future.*
> *Hear, within my own breast,*
> *The fluttering of the homeless bird, which,*
> *In company with countless others,*
> *Flies day and night,*
> *Through light and darkness,*
> *From shore to shore unknown.*
> *The void of the universe is resounding with the*
> *music of wings:*
> *Not here, not here, somewhere, far beyond!*[63]

Wherever Tagore went, he was respected and admired as a master. Only England gave him a more lukewarm welcome on this latest visit, even though Tagore owed it so much—but events in India and his contemptuous rejection of his knighthood could not help but influence public opinion. He was on the other hand still welcomed enthusiastically in Germany. Clearly, the dissatisfied, shattered Germany of the Twenties, staggering from the effects of runaway inflation, was looking for a saviour. For a brief moment that was what Tagore appeared to be, with his austere appearance, flowing snow-white hair, and invocations of tolerance and peace. His lessons at the Schule der Weisheit (School of Wisdom) in Darmstadt almost unleashed a popular frenzy. Equally memorable was his visit to Latin America, especially for the long-lasting friendship that grew in Buenos Aires with the writer Victoria Ocampo. In Italy he was given a hero's welcome, carefully orchestrated by Mussolini, who attended a performance of one of Tagore's plays with the King. It was Romain Rolland who suggested to him that he had allowed himself to be used by the regime, which led him to repudiate Fascism in an open letter to the *Manchester Guardian*. In the Soviet Union, too, he was received with full honours, and the enthusiastic letters he wrote on his stay there at the height of the Stalinist era confirm that Tagore's political judgement was sometimes clouded by the optimism of his imagination.

Travelling did not prevent Tagore from participating in the cultural life of his country, or from expressing his ideas about Indian society. He founded a literary review, and gave lectures that touched on unusual or difficult subjects such as female emancipation, love, freedom. At the age of sixty-seven, he took up painting, and many of his subsequent journeys would include exhibitions of some of the many drawings and paintings he produced in his lifetime.

Among the many exhibitions organised as he went around the world, the one at the Galerie Pigalle in Paris, immortalised in many photographs, became the most famous after it was visited by celebrities from the worlds of art and high society such as Henri Rivière, Paul Valéry and Anna de Noailles. But the following month Tagore was already in Oxford, again moving between salons and university lecture theatres. Here he gave the Hibbert lectures, published in 1931 under the title *The Religion of Man*, on a complex and fascinating subject—the humanity of God and the divinity of man.

But there was no let-up in his creative activities. In a period crowded with engagements, new acquaintances and honours, he wrote what is perhaps, together with *Dak Ghar (The Post Office)*, his most unusual and successful play—*Raktakarabi (Red Oleanders)*. In a mysterious realm, ruled by an enigmatic and distant monarch, a beautiful young girl subverts the order of things and transforms the despotic king into a libertarian rebel. In the following years he wrote two novels of love and completed his last work of fiction, *Char Adhyay (Four Chapters)*, once again set in the militant world of the Indian independence movement. Political and social themes continued to alternate with reflections on the solitude and destiny of man.

THE FINAL SEASON

IN HIS LAST YEARS, Tagore wrote almost exclusively poetry. His health had deteriorated, and his mobility was gradually restricted, until almost the only travelling he did was between Santiniketan and Calcutta. The poetry collections of those years, such as *Senjuti* (*Evening Light*) and *Prantik* (*The Borderland*), reflect a slow evolution—the content becomes less emotional and more abstract, the language terser and more modern.

Tagore no longer visited political leaders—they came to see him. In 1934, Nehru visited Santiniketan and Rabindranath gave him a respectful welcome. Nehru's interest in the projects realised by Tagore would turn out subsequently to be crucial, as would that of Gandhi, who years later came to see him again at Visva-Bharati. The poet, who could feel life slipping away from him, entrusted the material and spiritual legacy of Santiniketan to the Mahatma. This was in 1940, the same year in which the Indian administration formally took over the running of Santiniketan.

On 14th April 1941, on Rabindranath's eightieth birthday, a solemn celebration was arranged at Santiniketan. Wishes came from all over the world, but it was a divided world, plunged in the bloodiest, most tragic war of all time. The old poet was now almost at the end and the essay he had written for the occasion was read for him. "As I look around I see the crumbling ruins of a proud civilization strewn like a vast heap of futility" was his final bitter warning. "And yet I shall not commit the grievous sin of losing faith in Man."[64] Soon afterwards he was taken to Calcutta, to the house in Jorasanko that he had never liked. Here he died on 7th August of that same year. A few days earlier he had dictated a few untitled poems, which he did not even have the strength to correct. Like Hesse, who ended his life with *The Creak of a Broken Branch*, so Tagore closed his with a reference to nature, in these lines:

The last sun of the last day
Uttered the question on the shore of the western sea,
In the hush of evening—
Who are you?
No answer came.[65]

MAN, NATURE
AND THE WORLD

FORESTS OF THE MIND

ALL THE BOOKS TAGORE WROTE, the lessons he gave, the journeys he undertook and the projects he initiated revolve around one great idea—that of rediscovering in the distant roots of the Indian tradition the secret of how to live in peace with our neighbours and how to combine that with other traditions and cultures. The key that opens the door of these secrets and leads the wanderer towards happiness is nature, the most sacred place of every pilgrimage, a place where the soul attains knowledge.[66] If men and women aspire to attain a condition of joy and serenity in the course of their lives, they will first have to rediscover, not only a love of nature, but the feeling that they themselves are an integral part of the natural world. Our relationship with nature pervades every moment of our lives, be it physical, aesthetic, moral or spiritual.

"The water," said Tagore, "does not merely cleanse a man's limbs, but it purifies his heart; for it touches his soul. The earth does not merely hold his body, but it gladdens his mind; for its contact is more than a physical contact, it is a living presence."[67]

This sense of profound communion with creation has equally profound roots in Indian culture. It is a civilisation, says Tagore, that was born in the forests, in vast areas of wilderness. The ancient inhabitants did not try to mark out their territory, but to live with what the surrounding environment offered. The main aim of existence was not to possess but to understand, to increase knowledge of the things with which they were surrounded and from which they drew sustenance. The primitive social forms have evolved, but the Indians' love of animals, birds, trees has remained—to a degree that may seem excessive to people of other nations. It has been nourished over the centuries by a kind

143

of hermitage called *tapovana*, which Tagore called the heart of India's social body. To achieve harmony between the spirit of man and the spirit of the world—that was the aim of the wise men who lived in the forests; and even when an urban civilisation formed in India, people still looked to the wise men in the woods and their vision of the world with admiration and respect.

TO EAT OR WATCH A FISH?

T HESE ARE THEMES to which Tagore returns in greater depth in his essay 'The Relation of the Individual to the Universe', which is included in *Sadhana*. In it, he compares the Western and Eastern attitudes to nature. "The West," he says, "seems to take a pride in thinking that it is subduing nature, as if we are living in a hostile world."[68] The West, in fact, clearly distinguishes between man, on one hand, and animals, plants and everything that belongs to nature on the other, almost as though man was not part of nature. When Tagore wrote this, he was already familiar with Europe and its literature, but this statement reflects a highly rationalistic interpretation of European thought, prevalent, perhaps, at the time in which he lived. An immaterial God has created a purely physical order, which we call nature, to which our bodies and senses belong, but not our spirits. The more we become detached from material things, therefore, the closer we get to God. That thinkers like Spinoza denied the existence of a transcendent God and even saw Him as being at one with nature itself, that the study and love of nature were also a considerable part of both classical and modern Western culture—from Lucretius to Saint Francis, Goethe and Wordsworth—is something that Tagore seems to have ignored, but essentially it does not matter. He is right when he distinguishes two fundamentally different approaches, even though with a thousand variations and connections, to the relationship man is able to establish with nature—one of exploitation and use and the other of contemplation and love. And there is no doubt that, in Europe, the former ended by prevailing over the latter. In his passionate defence of the love of nature, Tagore, like Hesse, was a remarkable precursor of certain feelings and moral codes that would become established only many decades later. The two opposite visions man may have of nature—predatory and joyful—are nicely illustrated by a little story Tagore tells in *Sadhana*. Two men are watching a large fish swimming freely in the water. One is thinking that the fish belongs to a silent world full of joy and of life, while the other is thinking how nice it would be to eat it—and, Tagore comments, missing the point.[69]

The contradiction of the man who destroys that divine, joyful essence that is nature and, in so doing, creates his own unhappiness and destroys God, is a thought that surfaces often in Tagore and becomes ever more insistent with his advancing years. In his last poems we frequently find references to advanced technology and the machines that are taking over the world. He sees the railway stations, the puffing trains packed with people, hears the roar of bombs in a new war setting the world ablaze, watches the planes crossing the luminous skies of Bengal where once there were only clouds and birds:

In the brutal roaring of an aeroplane we hear
Incompatibility with sky
Destruction of atmosphere.[70]

Tagore understood that not even India, where nature had always been an integral part of culture, religion and life, would escape this gradual blight—that the fields would be replaced by concrete houses and the forests by factories. He foresaw the very thing about which enlightened Indian writers such as Arundhati Roy, Amitav Ghosh and Anita Desai are now raising the alarm—that his India and his Bengal would become increasingly distanced from nature and drift into the same decline that was affecting the whole world. One of his last thoughts in the final days of his life was of the grace of a fragile *simul* tree, glimpsed from the window of his last house at Santiniketan.

AN ABIDING LOVE

R ABINDRANATH LOVED NATURE even before he experienced it. Calcutta, where he was born, is one of the most densely populated cities in the world, with endless streets and immense neighbourhoods—it might be said that nowhere on earth is nature more remote. In the great patrician home of the Tagores at Jorasanko the boy Rabindranath felt like a prisoner. He had many brothers and sisters with whom he had to share his mother's affection and his father's casual attentions. The servants, to whom he was entrusted during the day, found it easier to keep him in the house than take him out. He could do nothing but dream of the outside world, which he only knew through words. It is a feeling that Tagore depicts wonderfully in one of his finest plays, *The Post Office*. A sick young man sees the world only in the postcards that arrive every now and again from the post office. One day, he hopes, the post office, which for him is the world, will have a postcard for him, too. And so the years pass by, and he remains confined to his house, vainly waiting for a postman to come to him from the outside world.

In the Jorasanko house there was a courtyard with a large banyan tree. That, for Rabindranath, was the world; that tree was nature. He never saw nature in the open air, he says in his memoirs, but only from his hiding place. It may be because he had longed for it so desperately that nature later became, for Tagore, the great source of salvation and happiness, the goal that each person unceasingly pursues in life.

His first real encounter with nature may have been belated, but, when it came, it left an indelible impression on him, being at the same time an encounter with freedom and spirituality.

147

Rabindranath was twelve years old, an imaginative boy but with very poor marks at school, when his father took him on a long journey without any particular aim, first through Bengal, then across the Punjab and all the way to the slopes of the western Himalayas. Their first stop was Santiniketan, and it was almost as if an inheritance were being bequeathed—on that same reddish land, which his father had seen almost by chance while visiting a friend ten years earlier and had bought in order to make it a place of meditation and prayer, Tagore was to create, years later, his greatest projects; it would become, indeed, the centre of his life. Now, at Santiniketan, young Rabindranath was finally allowed to run free; allowed to see, for the first time, a sunrise, a sunset, the horizon. The journey continued, and not everything was play. At Bakrota, near Dalhousie, in a small house in the mountains, before the sun rose, the father would give his son Sanskrit lessons and sing verses from the Upanishads, which the boy listened to in silence. Then came the hour for English, then the afternoon lessons, and in the evening the two would sit on the veranda and the father would point to the stars and tell his son their names. As they went from place to place, the journey became the first really constructive learning experience the boy had had—Tagore said once of school that he remembered the form more than the content—and a kind of spiritual initiation. It was an unusual itinerary and an unusual experience for Rabindranath, in which a wide variety of knowledge was imparted to him by his father, according to somewhat obscure criteria—among the books his father had with him, Tagore recalled, were not only classical and religious texts but also some unlikely works of history, such as several volumes of Edward Gibbon's monumental *The History of the Decline and Fall of the Roman Empire*. But for young Rabindranath the greatest discovery of the journey was nature. And by the time he returned to Calcutta four months later, he had, in a certain sense, become a man.

When a passion for nature enters our lives, there is no space that is not filled with it. In England, Rabindranath would look out of the window of his room in Bloomsbury at the grey skies, the cold clouds chasing one another, the bare trees. In Brighton, he saw the beaches covered with a white blanket of snow on which the waves broke. Still in his teens, the young man was discovering not only a new climate, but a new world. Soon after his return to India, he spent an enchanted time with his brother and his sister-in-law Kadambari. In his passionate memoirs of those days that were like a waking dream, nature takes the form of water: "The Ganges again! Again those ineffable days and nights, languid with joy, sad with longing, attuned to the plaintive babbling of the river along the cool shade of its wooded banks. This Bengal sky full of light, this south breeze, this flow of the river, this right royal laziness, this broad leisure stretching from horizon to horizon and from green earth to blue sky, all these were to me as food and drink to the hungry and thirsty. Here it felt indeed like home, and in these I recognised the ministrations of a mother."[71]

There, sitting on the bank in all his regal idleness, Rabindranath would watch the river flow by and feel an immense sense of repose covering the earth and reaching up to the sky. There, the days passed "like so many dedicated lotus blossoms floating down the sacred stream".[72] There, he was truly happy.

Nature, though, is not only contemplation, image or dream. It is life, it creates life and is necessary for life. When Tagore, at his father's behest, undertook his first experience of work, as chief administrator of the family estates to the east of Calcutta (in what is now Bangladesh), he chose to live in the closest way to nature that he could think of—on a boat on the river. His floating home, to which he gave the name *Padma*, from a branch of the Ganges delta, allowed him to move about in that labyrinth of land and water, to reach remote villages, to check on the state of the crops, and to spend the night close to the humble dwellings of the peasants. He did not consider himself an authoritarian *zamindar*, directing and deciding things from the outside. Rather, he felt himself to be almost one of them, one of the many creatures populating that boundless land, a part of the simple, humble soul of India.

How effective an administrator of those estates Rabindranath was, we do not know. What we do know is that his absence from Calcutta and from the temptations of public life inspired some of the most beautiful things he wrote in this early period of his work—a series of reflections in the form of a letter to a beloved niece named Indira, subsequently collected under the title *Glimpses of Bengal*, some short stories inspired by rural life, and a cycle of poems with the evocative title *Sonar Tari* (*The Golden Boat*). There is not a single page of *Glimpses of Bengal* that is not a quite tribute to the landscapes of Bengal, the scent of its grass, the green of its fields, the white of its sands, all expressed with the skill of a true writer, but also with the simplicity of someone who really loves the things he is talking about. The view of that infinite merging and diverging of water and earth—the thousand waterways vanishing and reappearing, the thousand islands, all the same and yet all different, that form the vast Ganges delta—suggests a metaphor to Tagore—that the river is like man, or like the whole of mankind, which moves ever forward, from the source where it is born to the sea where it dies, and that, between one mystery and another, there lies life, with its intrigues, its toil, its games, its constant chatter.

NATURE IS THE BEST SCHOOL

TAGORE'S DISCOVERY OF NATURE, as we have seen, was both fortuitous and liberating. He was like a bird born and raised in a cage that, as soon as the door of the cage is accidentally left open, flies away, however uncertain and confused at first. Thinking back on his unhappy childhood, he said that without a knowledge and love of the natural world no one can ever hope to attain harmony with what surrounds him, and, through it, happiness. When he had the idea for an educational project at Santiniketan that would lead the young to knowledge through joy instead of through compulsion and pain, intimacy with nature was, of course, an essential element. It is nature, and not an abstract discipline, that should dictate the first rules of conduct—the answers to a child's questions come, first and foremost, from the world about them. Natural things, in addition, have the merit of simplicity—to rise at dawn, to take care of one's own house and oneself, to do physical exercise to train the body and prayers and meditation to train the mind. Some activities practised at Santiniketan appear extraordinarily innovative even today, such as those designed to encourage the development of the senses, to increase the capacity to see, to listen, to interpret the signals that come to us from the plants and animals. There were long walks in the countryside, on which the children were taught to observe the peasants' way of life and subsistence, to see the landscape changing with the change of the seasons, or to look out for signs that the rains were coming. During the years spent on the *Padma*, Tagore had had a chance to observe the strict and cruel educational system prevalent in Bengali schools—the corporal punishment applied with bamboo sticks to the back, the repetitive, pointless writing exercises. The sadder he felt about his own school experience and that of the many young Bengalis he observed, the more determined he became to create a school which led, through nature, to happiness.

If we open a page of one of Tagore's many collections of poetry at random, we are almost certain to find a certain religious or spiritual feeling sometimes explicit, sometimes implied. Similarly, there are few poems without some reference to nature, in an adjective, a comparison, an image, a figure of speech. W B Yeats wrote in his introduction to *Gitanjali* that poetry and religion are the same thing in Tagore; but it could equally be said that nature and religion are the same thing in the Indian tradition, and therefore also in Tagore. It is hardly surprising, then, that the natural world is not only present in his poetry, but that it constitutes, together with religion, one of its main themes. Because of his thematic preoccupations, and the great facility with which he composed—almost improvised—his verses, the poet Tagore was compared to a *baul*, the wandering minstrel of Asia, who sings of the mountains and rivers that he crosses, the fruits and flowers he picks, the skies that he sees, and in so doing sings the praises of God. Tagore's God does not live in enclosed spaces, but in the stars and in the waters and fields of his land. Enclosed spaces suggest sadness and constraint, open places joy and freedom. "We may not know exactly what is happening," Tagore writes. "We do not know exactly even about a speck of dust. But when we feel the flow of life in us to be one with the universal life outside, then all our pleasures and pains are seen strung upon one long thread of joy."[73]

An image thrown out almost casually, but one of extraordinary vividness and seductiveness—the weft of the days, with the long thread of hope and suffering it carries with it, passes through the warp of nature and joy and thus creates the texture of life.

IN PRAISE OF TREES

IN RABINDRANATH TAGORE'S natural cosmogony, trees are leading actors. They are so because of their beauty, the variety of
their colours and the shapes of their leaves, their shade which
gives shelter and rest to the traveller and conveys a message of
peace to the anxious, their roots which sink into the earth from
which they draw sustenance, as if to indicate the profound unity
between everything, living or inanimate, on the planet, but above
all because, although trees are strong, they do not impress with
their strength as much as with their patience. This idea of trees is
very similar to that expressed by Hermann Hesse, and we find it
again in a long poem by Tagore actually entitled *In Praise of Trees*,
from the cycle *Bana-Bani* (*The Message of the Forest*):

> *O profound,*
> *Silent tree, by restraining valour*
> *With patience, you revealed creative*
> *Power in its peaceful form.*[74]

Nature, as we know, is not always kind and gentle. Tagore
does not describe it only in charming tones, nor does his world
consist only of colourful flowers and spring breezes. Bengal is
also a land of disasters, of torrential rains and winds that sweep
away houses and harvests. Bengal is no Garden of Eden, and
Tagore is well aware of that when he sings of its beauty. What is
beautiful is the great unity of the world, in which all things come
together—the monsoon season follows scorching summers, the
bad takes the good by the hand, and death embraces life in
the great round dance of the universe. Neither the good nor

the bad are immutable. One follows the other, and then the other surpasses it, and man cannot help but accept that eternal flow with serenity. This is the harmony that is attained when we abandon ourselves to the current of a river and Tagore feels that "the same stream of life that runs through my veins night and day runs through the world and dances in rhythmic measures".[75]

Tagore, of course, was not the only person to say that the law of the cosmos is a law of eternal movement. Many have done so, beginning with Heraclitus. "Die and become," wrote Goethe in a famous poem in his *West-East Divan*.[76] But in the Indian tradition, as in other Eastern cultures, the fear of death is less deep-rooted than in the western tradition. Instead of being in conflict, life and death complement one another—one cannot exist without the other. This, perhaps, is one of the most consolatory thoughts that Tagore offers us, and it is summed up in two verses of a poem from *A Flight of Swans*:

> *Between Life and Death*
> *There must somewhere be a harmony;*
> *Otherwise the world*
> *Could not have borne through the ages,*
> *Smiling, such a cruel deceit.*[77]

FROM DESERT TO GARDEN

IN TAGORE, thought is never an end in itself. He did not limit his own reflections, be they philosophical, educational or social, to verbal expression. For Tagore, words were not enough—he always tried to realise them in a concrete form. He certainly did so with his message that communion with the natural world is a stage on man's path towards happiness. Unlike Hesse, though, he did not become a gardener. Gardening, like working in the fields, requires a settled life. It was perfectly suited to Hesse who, for years on end, did not go further than a few miles from his own house and his own garden. Tagore, as we have seen, spent months, sometimes whole years, travelling—if he himself had had to tend to his garden, it would soon have turned to scrub. He therefore channelled this conviction into a project that was less manual and more ambitious.

When his father had first gone to Santiniketan, there was nothing to be seen on that vast expanse of land except two *chatim* trees—a shady plant that the English, for some reason, call the 'devil tree'. A few decades later, Rabindranath decided to transform that barren red terrain into a vast garden, so that the young people who studied there and teachers who taught there could feel happy. It was a colossal task, which remains uncompleted to this day. His father had made a start, improving the existing earth with mould brought from the forest. But, from a botanical point of view, it was land that had hardly known the hand of man—a few creepers on the walls and gate greeted the traveller coming from the south, a few coconut palms had grown in the western part and a few mangoes in the east. If that same traveller then sat down on the stone seat in

155

the shade of the *chatim* and looked northwards, he would not have seen anything green within sight, just open, uncultivated fields. The climate at Santiniketan is one of extremes. Summer is from April to June, when the temperature often climbs above forty degrees and a dry wind raises clouds of dust. Then comes the rainy season, when four-fifths of the annual rainfall falls between July and September. Winter is cold and dry, and only the mid-seasons have a temperate climate. Rabindranath set about planning and organising, bringing in water where it was needed and stabilising the topsoil. Then the planting began— trees for shade and fruit, local plants and plants from far away. From his journeys, Tagore would return with plants that were, in Indian terms, exotic—bougainvillea from Argentina, roses from China, chrysanthemums from Japan. To indicate the sacred character of the act of bedding out a plant and making it grow where it could develop the strength it had within itself, he created a tree-planting ceremony, which, eighty years later, is still repeated at regular intervals. It is a festive ritual, accompanied by music, dancing and singing. A young tree is borne on a palanquin and placed in the ground, while pupils from the school play the roles of the elements—water, light, earth, air—which will make it an adult plant.

With a great deal of determination and effort, Rabindranath Tagore's dream of creating a universal centre of knowledge, where people of every race and religion could study, teach and learn the highest expressions of thought and art was realised. Today, more than a hundred years since it was founded, starting life as a school and later, in 1921, becoming a large university, the institution still prospers, welcoming thousands of young people every year, although its influence has not spread in the way that Tagore hoped it would. The village of Santiniketan has lost some of its rarefied spirituality since the well-to-do classes of Calcutta started building second homes there. But his idea of making a splendid garden out of a barren piece of earth could not have met with greater success. Today, Santiniketan is a botanical paradise. On its open spaces, interspersed with buildings that range from what looks like a Japanese temple to a simple house made from blocks of mud, we find banyans, tamarinds, rubber trees and eucalyptus. The *asoka*—a tree whose brightly coloured flowers greatly impressed the first foreigners who saw it—grows beside the sacred fig. And among so many unknown bushes, a European will recognise the oleander and the jasmine, and amid so many low grasses, currants and gooseberries. Unlike Hesse, who tilled the earth with his own hands and planted every plant himself, Tagore had men working for him and, after a while, the help of his son Rathindranath and daughter-in-law Pratima—an agriculturalist and expert gardener respectively. His, though, was always the broad vision. In his garden, as in everything in his life, he was able to unite the sensibility of a poet with the temperament of an organiser.

In truth, if by the word 'garden' we mean those eminently decorative rectangles of earth of varying sizes that we find in every town on every continent, in which millions of owners plant whatever species can survive the local climate and brighten their outlook, then the word does not suit what Tagore created. Santiniketan is in fact a vast space, where buildings, roads, trees, grasses and flowers strive to create not a single aesthetic or functional ideal, but a sum total of many different ideals belonging to different cultures, historical periods, traditions and countries. If we look at the many buildings scattered about that vast area, we find some based on models from the Far East, some that echo archaic Indian structures, others inspired by the West but of disparate styles, from the classical to the modern, and so on. The same is true of the plants, which are not thrown together haphazardly, but arranged to represent the unity that holds together the infinite realities of the world. Santiniketan is a space designed to serve, not a single man or a single project, but many young people and many projects, as demonstrated by the twelve specialised libraries flanking a great central library containing many millions of volumes. Putting the source of knowledge within a garden is an assertion of the connection between the garden and man, between nature and the human mind.

It is also a reminder of the respect due by man to nature and the environment, the duty he has to preserve and defend its identity and infinite multiplicity. This duty lies at the root of the festivals and ceremonies which Tagore instituted at Santiniketan, and which are still held there. There are two kinds of festivities—the celebratory, related to religion or man-made events, and the propitiatory, connected to natural events—the seasons of the year, the winds, the times of planting. The alternation of these two kinds recalls the indissoluble, fertile, reassuring connection between man and nature in the unified balance of our universe.

Just as nature is not always benevolent, it is not always eye-catching or proud. The vegetable world does not consist only of imposing trees or brightly coloured flowers—there are also thousands and thousands of species that may seem insignificant and go unnoticed. But the world includes them too—it includes all humble things. To conclude this look at Tagore's reflections on nature here is a passage that restates his vision of an overall harmony where all things, large and small, have their place. "The grass has to put forth all its energy to draw sustenance from the uttermost tips of its rootlets simply to grow where it is as grass; it does not vainly strive to become a tree; and so the earth gains a lovely carpet of green. And, indeed, what little of beauty and peace is to be found in the societies of men is owing to the daily performance of small duties, not to big doings and fine talk."[78]

THE WAY TO THE WEST

FOLLOWING THE COURSE OF THE SUN

IN EXAMINING THE STAGES OF HESSE'S LIFE, we saw that over the years, while his body remained in its green refuge in the canton of Ticino, his mind gradually migrated eastwards in search of a spirituality that the West had lost. In this, Hesse was not the first to do so. Quite apart from Goethe and his *West-East Divan*, many Europeans, especially during the Romantic period, harboured the dream that there was an unexplored source of harmony and transcendence in the East.

This searching in the other half of the world for what one's own half has lost, or has never known, is one of the mirror characteristics of Hesse and of Tagore. While Hesse was static and travelled only in his mind, Tagore was dynamic and travelled in mind and body. Although deeply rooted in Indian culture and feeling great solidarity with it, he was attracted by the culture of the West or, at least, by certain aspects of that culture. He had a complex relationship with the West and, when tackling this theme in his essays and speeches, he sometimes contradicted himself. But he never questioned the idea that a new vision of the world, able to give every nation and every human being the possibility of attaining higher levels of harmony and serenity, can only grow out of the wisdom and experience of both cultural traditions.

Besides, Tagore had a taste for the West in his blood. His grandfather Dwarkanath amassed a great fortune by collaborating with the British East India Company, to the point that he owned mansions, factories and mines and was able to adopt an opulent, princely lifestyle. He also did something that, for a high-caste Indian in the middle of the nineteenth century, was so unusual as to be almost scandalous. He twice visited England, apparently earning the respect of Queen Victoria. While in England he died suddenly, leaving three children, a great deal of property, and a lot of debts. The family continued partly to squander the fortune and partly to rebuild it, maintaining ties with Great Britain and introducing Western implements, objects and even, to some extent, ways of life into their homes. In the house in Calcutta where Rabindranath grew up, there were Italian paintings, and the flute, the violin and the piano were played at family gatherings—with what musical results we have no way of knowing. Even the prayer room of the Brahmo-Samaj association, to which Tagore's grandfather and father, and then Rabindranath himself, devoted so much effort, boasted a pipe organ as testimony to the religious freedom that inspired its principles.

It is hardly surprising, therefore, that, in Rabindranath's somewhat haphazard intellectual development, Western, and especially English literature, poetry and thought, occupied an important and perhaps pre-eminent place. It is possible that, in taking his young son with him on a journey of initiation across India, Tagore's father hoped, without renouncing the West, to acquaint him with the aesthetic and religious roots of his country. As the years passed, he would continue to enlarge his reading, and by the time he was an adult, his knowledge of literature, philosophy and history equalled that of any sophisticated Western intellectual.

Rabindranath had a great love of Shakespeare, and among poets he especially admired the Romantics—Byron, Keats, Shelley. Later, he became very fond of Walt Whitman, in whom he recognised the same passionate love of nature, even in its humblest manifestations, as he himself had. He also knew other European literatures. With the small amount of German he had learnt, he tried to translate a few poems by Heinrich Heine, and even attempted to read Goethe's *Faust* in the original language but, as he himself admitted, he did not understand much of it. Tagore's idea of the West, however, did not come only from books. As we have seen, he travelled a great deal to America and Europe. In his lifetime, he met many people from many different countries and the most diverse strata of society. He mixed with literary figures such as Ezra Pound, W B Yeats and Victoria Ocampo, politicians and members of the European aristocracy, and all of them were happy, especially after he had been awarded the Nobel Prize, to meet him, talk to him and have their picture taken with him. Among them was Albert Einstein, with whom Tagore had some fascinating conversations, and records of some of them remain. One was about music and the relative value of the musical modes of East and West, another about the nature of beauty and truth. While in the former, both men found themselves to be basically in agreement, in the second they had opposing opinions. Tagore maintained that, if men did not exist, truth would not exist, while Einstein disagreed—but neither man was in a position to prove his own thesis.

Tagore, in other words, had every opportunity to build up an image of the Western world that was anything but superficial, unlike the average Indian of his time, who would have seen it above all through the distorting lens of British administrative and military domination. And yet his relationship with the West was ambiguous. On the one hand, he never tired of reminding the West that the frenetic race for a scientific progress whose ultimate aim is the possession or enjoyment of material possessions, while exacerbating the misunderstandings and conflicts between peoples (as the wars of the twentieth century would demonstrate), ends by reducing man to a material dimension. He always strove, in his lectures and in the various lessons he gave in universities, to introduce India, its history, its ancient civilisation and such basic principles of its spiritual tradition as tolerance and unity in diversity. He saw it as his task when in the West to preach the rediscovery of a broadly-based religious sense, not tied to the observance of a particular creed, and not separated from daily practice, of which in fact it is an integral part, within an overall vision of men's lives related to the cultural tradition of the East.

His relationship to Hinduism is centred on the *Upanishads* but, as a convinced advocate of ecumenism between different faiths, he recognised the validity of many of the principles of Christianity, even though the spiritual tradition to which he felt closest was perhaps that contained in the teachings of the Buddha. However, like Hesse's his was a very personal creed, gradually achieved over time, 'a poet's religion', as he himself often called it—essentially, a moral vision of the world expressed through music and poetry.[79] Tagore urges us to oppose hate with love, war with peace, division with unity, haste with slowness, noise with silence, and activity as an end in itself with meditation. This is the message contained in many essays and reflections later collected under various titles, both during his lifetime and after his death. It was a message already present in his first collection of poems, which he himself translated into English, and which earned him an international reputation. It is not without significance that the same Nobel committee that brought him fame had, a few years earlier, awarded their prize to Rudyard Kipling, a great writer who described India between the nineteenth and twentieth centuries with extraordinary talent, but who is almost a symbol of English colonial domination and someone who asserted that there was an unbridgeable gulf between the two worlds: "East is East, and West is West, and never the twain shall meet".[80]

A GREAT MEDIATOR

TAGORE'S LONG SEARCH for an existential choice capable of giving serenity and joy through the uplifting and maturing of the spirit was always combined with a strong sense of reality and a genuine need for industriousness and concreteness. It was this that led him to have a different attitude towards the West, which went hand in hand with the one we have so far examined.

Addressing Europeans, he urged them to overcome their fundamentally materialistic conception of man's needs, but later he warned his compatriots against the risk of converting a spiritual culture into an excuse for inertia. From the West, he said, came modernity, innovation and reason, the supremacy of science and a knowledge of the principles by which reality can be organised. An Indian, he wrote in a letter just before his second decisive journey to England in 1912, wonders why anyone born in India should ever travel beyond its borders. A European, on the other hand, would never ask himself such a question—for him travel is knowledge, it is an opportunity in which he can find what an Indian finds in a pilgrimage.[81] As for the pre-eminence of the spiritual over the material, there is no doubt that, seen from the East, Western civilisation appears fundamentally materialistic. But every great civilisation, he says, has a spiritual force behind it, and the fact that Western civilisation is advancing and progressing is a sign that it contains within it spiritual values which nourish it.

Tagore, in other words, was placing himself rationally between the two worlds. He did not question the supremacy of spirit over matter, but pointed out that they are not in conflict with each other, because they both belong to the same unity, the overall unity of the cosmos. Long before Europe, he says, India reached a very high level of civilisation, such a high level, in fact, as to create the feeling that it was perfect, that there was no need to explore any other culture. Because of this, inertia gradually took the place of industriousness. If the rain floods our streets—Tagore said once, speaking in Calcutta in defence of Annie Besant, an English social reformer who campaigned for Indian self-government and who had recently been interned by the British—we are not surprised, because we know that the wind brings rain and that in every season the streets are flooded. That was so when Tagore was a child and looked at the streets from the veranda of his house and it was still so fifty years later, when the goal of having a national government in India was starting to be within reach. If, on the other hand, said Tagore, you go to the Chowringhee district, where the Europeans live, you will see that the streets are not flooded and that pedestrians do not have to battle with the mud to cross them. The difference is that the Indians resign themselves and the Europeans do not, the Indians consider that nothing can change the course of things and the Europeans think the opposite. The conclusion of this argument was that it was up to the Indians to take charge of their own affairs, even at the risk of committing mistakes, emulating the determination and will of the Westerners and dismissing from their minds the thought, lodged there for centuries, that there was no point in trying to change the course of the world.[82]

It was, as we can see, a balanced judgement, which did not fail to arouse negative reactions in the most radical Indian nationalist circles. If, on the one hand, Tagore was asserting the right and duty of Indians to self-government, on the other he was maintaining that, in order to attain it, it was necessary to adopt certain principles of rules and discipline associated' with their English masters. This, essentially, lay at the root of his disagreement with the more militant forms of the *svaraj*, the political movement for independence, which Tagore theoretically supported. When, for example, some years later, Gandhi tried to persuade Tagore to support the form of non-violent resistance symbolised by the *charkha*, the primitive spinning wheel, which ought, according to the Mahatma, to be in every Indian household as a way of boycotting the import of textiles from British mills, Tagore smiled respectfully and shook his head. The future of India did not lie in a return to archaic ways of life or in exalting the symbols of poverty. That same poverty had sapped the country since time immemorial, and it could not be defeated only with handicrafts and manual work, while denying the achievements of science—it was necessary to learn and to educate. This, in Tagore's opinion, was the lesson his compatriots had to learn from the West, just as the Japanese has learnt it, without repudiating their own traditions. This, deep down, was also the reason he conceived and realised Visva-Bharati—not as an Indian university for Indians, but a university where scholars of every country could transmit their knowledge to young people from all over the world. A free, multicultural university where Indian culture and tradition, too, could be studied under foreign teachers—such famous European orientalists as the Frenchman Sylvain Levi and the Italian Giuseppe Tucci did, in fact, teach there. Such a balanced, realistic conception of the relationship between East and West—a long way from the arrogant superiority of that section of European culture that tends to see the profound spirituality of the East as an unproductive area of little importance; a long way, too, from the limited vision of those Indian nationalists who were concerned only for their own immediate objectives and rejected the qualities of their opponents—such a conception was not the result of chance but had formed in Tagore through a long maturing process, in which his ideas had been gradually broadening, like the ripples created by a stone thrown into water. One Indian scholar has distinguished four phases in this process. In the first phase, Tagore was mainly inspired by his native Bengal and its problems. In the second, he was influenced by the *svadesi* movement of national liberation. In the third, partly inspired by the pan-Asian message of his friend Kakuzo Okakura, he extended his reflections to the entire continent. And in the fourth and final phase, he was concerned not only with the needs and hopes of the Bengali, Indian or Eastern man, but with those of universal man and his universal aspiration to peace and happiness.[83]

THE CODE OF HARMONY

HAPPINESS IS EVERYWHERE

TAGORE WAS NOT A SYSTEMATIC THINKER, and his vision of the world was not a construction in which every element has a functional place and a predetermined design. In fact there are a number of contradictory aspects to his ideas, and others that evolved over the years. Some critics have pointed out the various cultural influences, while others have seen an undefined religious sense as the dominant element. Others, again, have found in his work a search for a higher level of knowledge that makes him a spiritual guide, a great master of life.

What is certain is that everything he said, did and wrote revolves around a central question—that of how to attain both universal harmony and peace between peoples and individual harmony and happiness. In reality, when Tagore speaks about happiness, he uses the Sanskrit word *ananda* and translates it into English as *joy*, which suggests more a state of mind than a response to external circumstances. His is a positive, affirmative vision of life, as long as we have eyes to look, ears to listen, and the desire to see both the reality in which we live and the reality beyond it. Even in suffering. Even in old age and in illness, says Tagore in a poem written in the last year of his life, when another "brutal night comes silently" and we feel "the shame of defeat/the insult of this fatigue" even then, at sunrise:

> *against the tranquil light of morning*
> *I see myself as a conqueror of sorrows,*
> *standing on top of my fortress, my ruin, my body.*[84]

171

Happiness, says Tagore, is everywhere. This is the subtlest, most profound message he left us. "Joy is there everywhere; it is superfluous, unnecessary; nay, it very often contradicts the most peremptory behests of necessity."[85] Happiness is within reach of every human being, at the top of a ladder whose rungs are the realisation of oneself, in inner seeking and outward action. Tagore distances it from the common notion (common not only in the Eastern world) that sees work mostly as a necessity. He sees it instead as joy and makes his ideas clearer through a comparison between work and the law. Many consider that the law is the opposite of joy, whereas it is actually when the soul is uncontrolled that it languishes and prepares its own ruin. Likewise, there are those who think that activity is the opposite of freedom, whereas it is in activity that the soul finds freedom and in work that it reflects itself and knows the world.

No animal, no creature in existence works as man does. Man does not work only out of necessity—he could satisfy his basic needs by working much less. Through activity man escapes inertia and darkness, through action and knowledge, he experiences immortality in this life. It is written in the *Upanishads* that only in the midst of activity does man wish to live for a hundred years. Life and activity are closely connected.[86]

The reference Tagore makes in this context to one of the greatest texts of the Indian religious tradition restores a concept of activity and work as not only necessary but elective component parts of life, a concept which belongs rather to a Western vision. Tagore then hastens, in the same essay, to warn against frenzied activity designed to assert one's own sense of power, which is an evil characteristic of the West. Doing, says Tagore, is a search for truth, it is putting oneself in tune with the harmony of the world, it is joy; otherwise it is only woe and toil.

GROWING OLD WITH A SMILE

J OY CAN BE THE COMPANION of any age of a man's life. Every
age, in fact, has its beauty, says Tagore, touching once again
on a theme that was equally dear to Hesse. We need to accept
old age, indeed we have to "welcome it as a guest".[87] When it
comes down to it, man is no different from a fruit—once a fruit
has ripened, it begins to shrivel on the outside, but remains sweet
inside, and its seeds prepare to create new life. More than any
other time of life, old age demands discipline and will, because
a new role awaits us. After the age of education, after the age of
work, old age is when we begin to change and loosen our earthly
bonds, it is what precedes the fourth and final phase of the life of
man, which is the wait for liberation through death. To change,
to transform is what Tagore himself did, remaining active and
creative to the end, even in the last decade of his life, when he
was frequently ill and racked with pain. In those years he con-
centrated on writing poetry—a poetry that was essential, concise
and often unpredictable, written in a dry, direct language close
to prose. This time of growing physical decline saw the creation
of some of the most elevated, most inspired works in his entire
poetic output. The collection *The Borderland* is a meditation on
the past and the present, the fragility of beauty and the causes
of suffering, written, as the title implies, from the edge of things.
When, in the 1930s, the institutions he had created experienced
increasing economic difficulties, the income from his publica-
tions in the West dwindled and his own reduced mobility pre-
vented him making any more long journeys around the world, he
and his students organised theatrical presentations, dances and
musical dramas to raise the funds necessary for the survival of

those institutions. At an age when most men have either already abandoned or are in the process of abandoning an active life, Tagore had the courage to express himself in a new artistic language, painting—something like two thousand paintings and drawings are his impressive legacy.

DOING AND CREATING

WHEN HESSE TALKS OF DOING, of activity, as an essential component of the state of serenity it is possible for men to attain, he is thinking above all of everyday work, the humble things which the powerful disdain but which are, in fact, the medicine that calms the anxieties and uncertainties of the spirit. Gardening is the most perfect expression of this because it combines activity with nature. Tagore also cites activity as one of the conditions necessary for human happiness: activity is the means by which a human being gets to know reality and makes it his own—only by acquiring that awareness can man realise himself and only when he has realised himself can he achieve a superior state of harmony and happiness. The highest level of activity, the extension of the borders of reality, of his understanding and realisation of himself, is attained through creative activity, such as art and literature. In creating a work of art, he says in *Personality*, a person selects "things from his surroundings in order to make them his own. He has his forces of attraction and repulsion by which he not only piles up things outside him, but creates himself."[88] Of course, Tagore admits, one's personality can also be realised in everyday work, when we act to satisfy our habits and our needs. In that case, however, we "are economical in our expression"[89] and the awareness that we have of ourselves is at a lower level. When, on the other hand, we feel that our need to express ourselves is an end in itself, then it becomes art, we forget the small necessities and restrictions of the useful and our spirit ("the spires of our temple")[90] reaches for the stars or descends into the depths of the unsayable. This is the theoretical construction, but, even before he had expressed it concisely, Tagore had already drawn concrete implications from it. We cannot all be poets or artists or painters. But we can all express ourselves in an activity that does not have a utilitarian end, thus realising a secret side of ourselves. Man does not express himself only through words—there are lines, colours, sounds, movements which he can use in order to be a fuller and more joyful part of the world. In the dominance of reason and language, characteristic of Western culture, he sees a clear limitation in the educational system and the whole academic culture inspired by the West. Countering this tendency may constitute an implicit, potential superiority of the East. Dance, Tagore tells us, sing, paint, do ceramics, carpentry, gardening, without any other purpose than to liberate, through play, your deepest dimension. In whatever direction your inclination leads you, give it free rein—you will be more complete and you will feel happier.

WHICH ART TO CHOOSE?

THAT IS WHAT TAGORE HIMSELF DID CONSTANTLY, in the most varied directions, throughout his life. By any normal standards, he would be considered versatile, moving as he did, almost casually, from poetry to novels, plays, essays and autobiographical writings, depending on his state of mind and the inspiration of the moment. But for a Bengali, the name of Tagore is most linked to his songs, the *Rabindrasangit*, for which he often also composed the music. In Indian music, singing has an essential function and derives from very ancient traditions, from the singing of mantras—mystical formulas—and religious hymns. Tagore was inspired by this musical and spiritual heritage to enrich it with his own output, which, as in every other field, was vast—two thousand five hundred songs in which words and music combine harmoniously. So popular and widespread in Bengal are his songs and so great is his reputation that even readings of his poetry in his native land are very often accompanied by music, so that his whole huge poetic oeuvre is transformed into song.

"Music is the purest form of art,"[91] writes Tagore in that inexhaustible treasure house of reflections on the destiny of man, *Sadhana*. But music is not only the purest, it is also the first form of art, dating back to the dawn of man, and Tagore would continue to consider it almost as the mother of every artistic expression. One summer near the end of his life, Tagore escaped the heat and went to stay in a village in the mountains near Darjeeling. Here, he dictated his childhood reminiscences, in which he speaks of his initiation into music when he was a child, and the lessons to which he did not pay

177

much attention, but also of the spell cast on him by the popular songs and music of Bengal and his interest in a well-known musician who often visited the family home. His beloved brother Jyotirindranath—"Jyotidada" as Rabindranath called him affectionately—with whom he would later spend some of the most memorable and crucial years of his intellectual development, was twelve years older than him and just as versatile as Rabindranath was subsequently to become. Tagore recalls with emotion the day on which a piano and some new varnished furniture arrived at the family home in Calcutta and his breast swelled with pride at such a display of modernity. His brother was soon able to play, and he would constantly be improvising new melodies in new keys. Rabindranath would try to adapt the words of his songs to those rapidly composed pieces, and in his heart his love for music and his love for his brother became one and the same.

If music was chronologically the first, painting was the last and most unusual bond Tagore had with the arts—a late bond, as we have already seen, in that he began painting when he was nearly seventy. He believed that young people should be trained to paint, but refused any formal training himself. He painted, or more often drew in pen and ink and then added colour, in a frenzy of pure self-expression. Here, too, as with literature and music, his imagination and capacity for work were inexhaustible, and the staggering quantity of works produced in a dozen years bear witness to a truly boundless energy.

What is most surprising, apart from the sheer mass of the work, is that it went in a completely different, indeed radically opposed direction to that which he pursued in his literary work. In his poetry, as in his prose, Tagore always kept to the model of beauty and harmony which he himself advocated and which he expressed faithfully in both content and style. His painting seems to come from a different world, as if it were the product of someone else's mind. His visual universe is dark, often anguished, his self-portraits cruel and grotesque, his figures disturbing, his landscapes crepuscular. Parallels could be drawn, with some justification, with certain styles of the European avant-garde, especially German Expressionism.

Were there two Tagores, then? One, serene and constructive, who invites us to follow him on the path of joy, the other, agitated and feverish, who can only free himself with the brush and the pencil and is destined to remain a secret? Even this hypothesis is contradicted by the fact that Tagore loved to show his paintings and took them with him on his last journeys in order to hold exhibitions in conjunction with his lectures.

Tagore was a man of contradictions, as he himself readily admitted. The anxious, tormented nature of his visual works must be classed as just one among his many inconsistencies.

NOT THIS LOVE

T HE ROADS THAT HERMANN HESSE and Rabindranath Tagore travelled to attain happiness, are, as we have seen, extraordinarily close, despite the fact that they started from such different personal experiences and environments. Both, almost within view of their destination, entered a territory that every man, and every woman, has inside their mind from the moment of birth—love. In Tagore, love is everywhere—in almost every line of his poems, on almost every page of his stories, novels and plays. All it takes is the jangle of a bracelet, a casual glance, a scent carried on the breeze, and thoughts of love are aroused.

> *You walked by the riverside path*
> *With the full pitcher upon your hip.*
> *Why did you swiftly turn your face*
> *And peep at me through your fluttering veil?*
> *That gleaming look from the dark came upon me*
> *Like a breeze that sends a shiver through the rippling water*
> *And sweeps away to the shadowy shore.*[92]

Often the loves recounted by Tagore are passionate, impetuous and, in his fiction, accompanied by references to the natural world—almost as if the thought of love, as soon as it is formulated, must immediately turn to the sky or to water in order to be real. In the novel *The Home and the World*, for example, this is how Bimala, a young woman attracted to the figure of a passionate, brave, arrogant hero of the independence movement, describes her feelings: "So long I had been like a small river at the border of a village. My rhythm and my language were different from what they are now. But the tide came up from the sea, and my breast heaved; my banks gave way and the great drumbeats of the sea waves echoed in my mad current."[93]

When we look more closely, however, it appears that love is present more in his pages than in his life. Despite the best efforts of his many biographers, we know nothing about any youthful loves he may have had. His marriage to little Mrinalini was arranged by his father, and Rabindranath agreed to it before he had even met his bride. It is hardly surprising that love had nothing to do with it—first comes marriage and then comes love, as many say in India even now, in contrast with what happens in the West, where love usually precedes marriage but often does not survive it. It is strange, though, that Tagore did not devote a line to Mrinalini in his memoirs, as if she had poured all of herself into her duties as a wife and there was nothing else to say about her.

The only love of Tagore's that is known, or at least suspected, is the love he felt for his sister-in-law Kadambari when he lived together with her and his brother Jyotirindranath. And even this remains a shadowy episode. Rabindranath admired Kadambari as a person who, as he wrote in his autobiography, "seemed not to have even the slightest fault in a thread of life closely woven with laughter and tears."[94] A beautiful but somewhat ambiguous expression, which other memories contained in the book do nothing to clarify. Tagore admired Kadambari's aesthetic sense, her exquisite refinement, her charm, her receptiveness. Then came the shock and grief at the apparently motiveless death of a beautiful young woman, a trauma that Tagore remembered even in the last days of his life. Whatever else there may have been, between the admiration and the grief, remains a matter of conjecture. The family did everything it could to make it seem as though her suicide was a natural death and, if nothing else, succeeded in ensuring that the episode was not talked about. Even Tagore preferred silence.

A third female figure in Tagore's life who could be vaguely associated with the word 'love' is the Argentinian intellectual

Victoria Ocampo. Today, Ocampo is best known for having introduced the world to the work of Jorge Luis Borges through her review *Sur*, but when Tagore met her she was already a tireless, attractive woman of letters in her thirties, who had befriended all the fashionable poets and writers of her time. Victoria offered Tagore hospitality in her villa not far from Buenos Aires when he fell ill on his journey to Latin America in 1924. He not only accepted the invitation, but remained her guest for almost two months, until he left for Italy. Victoria Ocampo was a proud, aristocratic, sensual and vain woman (that is how Leonard K Elmhirst, who accompanied Tagore on that particular journey, describes her) and although she already had a husband and a lover, she may well have wanted to add this rare specimen from the East to her collection. Here, too, we have to rely on a great deal of conjecture. Rabindranath himself did not clarify his feelings until he had left, writing Victoria a long letter from the ship that was taking him away across the Atlantic: "Whenever there is the least sign of the nest becoming a jealous rival of the sky, my mind, like a migrant bird, tries to take its flight to a distant shore" ... I tell you all this because I know you love me."[95] And so, making it clear that his destiny was to be involved with ideas and not human beings, he rejected the nest that Victoria Ocampo was offering him in Argentina and resumed his travels from one continent to another.

The love which Tagore had in mind, the love which opens the way to happiness was, obviously, neither his probably imaginary love for Kadambari, nor Victoria's essentially tyrannical love for him. That would have been the case even if the former had been real and the latter had been mutual, because he was not talking about love for a single person or a single thing. It is love for all creatures and for all things or rather (given how difficult it is to love everyone and everything passionately) a disposition to love all creatures and all things. When this love finds fulfilment, the feeling of separation between oneself and others vanishes, the mind of man overcomes the limits which nature has set on it, crosses the threshold of the infinite and feels that it is at one with the whole. "Therefore love," he writes, "is the highest bliss that man can attain to."[96]

In saying this, Tagore is making two complementary points. Firstly, that in love we feel we are part of something infinitely bigger, part of a whole. Secondly, that only through this feeling can we be happy. The world is made up of opposites, positive and negative elements, forces that attract and repel. Even if they go in opposite directions, such forces are not in conflict and are reconciled in a 'rhythmic dance' in the harmony of the universe. It is the same image we find in Hesse, although in different words—the unity which encapsulates the manifold, something our mind finds difficult to explain but can sense. "The mystery of all mysteries," as Tagore defines it, or else a "sublime paradox".[97] It is love that draws us into this mystery and, since the feeling that the ego is transcending itself produces joy, love is a source of joy and happiness.

To raise himself towards the divine, he writes in *The Religion of Man*, man has no need of temples or mosques, sacred symbols or religious rituals. In fact, temples and mosques, wise priests and angry masters hinder the path upwards because whoever obeys the voices of others no longer hears his own. It is within himself that man must search to find divinity. A calm inner search, a solitary path towards heaven, is what Tagore hears in the *baul*, the wandering minstrel of Bengal (some compared Tagore himself to a *baul*). The *baul* expresses himself through song, which is his form of religion and prayer and, through it, expresses love. This, he wrote, is the magic stone that transforms desire into sacrifice and ensures that heaven becomes earth and God becomes man.

As Tagore well knew, the great religious traditions of India are not alone in admonishing us for putting our egos at the centre of the universe, or in urging us to disregard personal gain and to show compassion and love for others. This message can be found in the *Upanishads*, and in the teachings of the Buddha, but also, in more general terms, in the Christian precept of love for one's neighbour. And it was in two men of a different faith and with different backgrounds from his own, that he saw a concrete embodiment of the Christian message—two missionaries who worked in India but whom he met during his journey to England in 1912. Charles Freer Andrews and William Winstanley Pearson were both involved in charitable works in that vast receptacle of human misery called Calcutta, and also looked sympathetically on those who were committed to the wider effort to restore dignity and autonomy to the whole of India. Both men had been in contact with Gandhi in South Africa, and Andrews, on a number of occasions, acted as an intermediary between the Mahatma and Tagore in the years that followed. They both became part of the Santiniketan project. Tagore was particularly fond of Andrews, and had enormous admiration for his generous, disinterested charitable work, even mentioning him in his last ever public speech—entitled *Crisis in Civilisation*.

We cannot love what we do not know, and we cannot be happy if we do not love—that is Tagore's message—a message that goes beyond the individual and can be adopted by the whole of society, because love must also be the essential element in the conduct of nations and those who govern them. A civilisation, Tagore maintains, is not judged by the level of power it has reached, or the vastness of the territory it has occupied, or the nations it has subjugated, but by the way in which it demonstrates, through its laws, its love of humanity. Just as there is no dividing line within man between the physical and the spiritual, because both combine and are reconciled in the unity of being, so there is no line separating what belongs to the individual from what belongs to everyone. Our gestures of love do not touch only a single individual, they touch the whole world.

ANCIENT WISDOM,
MODERN SCIENCE

APPRENTICESHIP IN HAPPINESS

MEN AND WOMEN of every age and condition continue to visit the places where Rabindranath Tagore lived and the museum that houses mementoes of Hermann Hesse. When I saw those long lines of people waiting to go in, I was surprised by their number. And yet it is only a small percentage of the much larger number of people who have found their writings to be a source of support, and a guide to the difficult task of living. However different in scale and content, their works share a single great basic message—happiness is neither a right nor a gift, but something that can be attained through a process of learning and achievement. Men are not equal—the external conditions under which they live and their inner conditions of aptitude and temperament may be extremely different. There are those whose lot in life has been pain and suffering, and others who have enjoyed good health and a comfortable lifestyle. There are also those who are afflicted by mental disorders that make choice impossible, and which can only be cured with medicine and drugs. But the people we call 'normal', those who are in a position to think for themselves and decide what they want, can consciously work to go from suffering to a state of well-being, or increase that well-being if they already have it and become happy. We need a long, patient apprenticeship, say Hesse and Tagore, and we need to educate ourselves in happiness. When they said this, European thought was running along very different lines—the way to improve men's lot, it was believed, was to deal with their external conditions, through the mastery of science (as the heirs of positivism maintained) or through the levelling of society (as the heirs of Engels and Marx asserted).

And yet the idea that man's lot depends primarily on himself and that the attainment of happiness is above all an inner act, an autonomous spiritual journey quite different from the beliefs and promises of religion, has been present, in both West and East, since ancient times. Happiness is a mental state that can be attained through practice, the pre-Socratic philosophers claimed. There were philosophical schools in ancient Greece that practised actual 'therapeutic' exercises—procedures through which men could learn to reject destructive feelings and generate positive ones. For Aristotle, too, a happy life was the result of human conduct—happy is the man who lives virtuously, and to be virtuous we have to become accustomed to practising virtue until it becomes second nature.

As for the East, the teachings of Buddhism (and those even older) posit happiness as the ultimate goal of man; and since one cannot be happy and unhappy at the same time, it is above all necessary to reject those things that disturb our minds—vain or unsatisfiable desires, fear, enmity and the spirit of revenge. On the level of positive action, what brings man closer to a happy state is love and compassion for others. Both these actions, the rejection of negative feelings and the creation of positive ones, are made easier by the learning of appropriate techniques, one of which is meditation. Happiness, or whatever comes closest to it, is not the result of chance but of a conscious effort on the part of the individual.

The vision Hesse and Tagore had of man's path and destiny had been anticipated thousands of years before by some illustrious predecessors in both East and West. It has since received unexpected confirmation from a number of scientific and statistical studies of human happiness many decades after their deaths.

In some large universities in the United States, a branch of psychology has emerged known as 'positive psychology', which by interpreting feelings which are widespread at every level of our society, asserts that a positive, altruistic attitude to reality is not only part of our genetic legacy, but is an attitude that can be deliberately acquired and developed, and the earlier this is done the better the result. This is the theme of Tal Ben-Shahar's Harvard courses on happiness, self-esteem and creativity; it is also the central idea, as the title *Learned Optimism* indicates, of a book by Martin E P Seligman, a prolific writer and scholar, and one of the best known contemporary American psychologists. Studies in the fields of biology, physics and medicine have also confirmed the accuracy of Hesse's and Tagore's insights. A German biophysicist, Stefan Klein, author of another book that has become very popular, entitled *The Science of Happiness*, maintains that the state of the body directly influences the state of the mind, and underlines the importance of movement and activity for the well-being of the latter. Klein does not deny that internal and external factors can influence our mental condition—having good health, social order, and a sense of community and peace are all conditions that contribute to happiness, but are not in themselves sufficient without the contribution of the individual's will and actions. Klein's theories, and those of others who, like him, have examined the subject of happiness through the prism of science, are based on the most recent studies on the workings of the brain and the neurotransmitters that carry external sensations to the brain, creating the mechanisms of memory, pleasure and pain, and therefore also of happiness and unhappiness.

Last but not least, the fields of economics and economic statistics have also begun to confirm that individual well-being is only partly, and in a limited way, the product of external material circumstances. The 'humanistic' school of economics, of which the Nobel Prize winner Amartya Sen—educated at Santiniketan—is a proponent, has studied the reactions of various categories of people to variations in economic and social conditions over a period of time. Richard Layard, an English economist of this school, has demonstrated how the increase in wealth that the West has experienced in the last few decades has, paradoxically, not been matched by a corresponding growth in feelings of satisfaction and of well-being but, on the contrary, an increase in dissatisfaction, which results in anxiety, stress, aggression, violence, family breakdown, loss of values and so on. Layard uses these findings to argue that, even in the sphere of politics and government, we should go back to a model that takes moral values into account as primary and irreplaceable elements of existence. In so doing, and coming from a completely different direction, he corroborates the idea that happiness is the result of immaterial as well as material conditions—the product of the human being's patience, humility and willingness to learn and to act.

A DIFFERENT LOOK

How, in concrete terms, human beings should act, what actions they should undertake and what companions they should choose in their journey towards happiness, has been the theme of this book. Hesse and Tagore, without ever meeting or corresponding, arrived at very similar, sometimes identical ideas on the path mankind should follow and on how each individual should steer his own course in order to overcome adversity and reach his final goal. Time has increasingly confirmed their claims and many of their views are shared today by the most sensitive and alert strata of our society.

Think, for example, of nature. Both Hesse and Tagore saw it as a central point of reference in man's existence, an object of love, care and daily practice; and both often proclaimed, each in their own way, that the preservation of the environment and a respect for nature are essential for the well-being of the collective and the happiness of the individual. This has now become one of the most topical of all subjects, much debated by politicians, businessmen and ordinary members of the public—even though it often happens that individuals do not practise what they preach.

They not only wrote about principles but adhered to them, Hesse in his industrious, patient passion for gardening and in his long solitary walks, Tagore by making it a subject to be taught. Both also chose to live in places where nature was nearby, and very visible, in small towns far from the congestion and uproar of the big cities.

The restless German writer self-exiled to Switzerland and the versatile Indian poet who travelled the world both sensed that wars, revolutions and the growing violence of their times would drive men in search of calm towards the immutable laws of nature. During the age of the city states, when every town was in conflict with its neighbour, the gardens of the monasteries, created not for ornament but for survival, were places of peace and meditation. It was in the turbulent Europe of the Napoleonic and post-Napoleonic eras, ravaged by clashing armies and equally clashing ideas, that the notion of a new kind of garden was born, a garden inspired by the natural landscape and completely different from the formal French and Italian gardens of previous centuries. Hesse and Tagore, who had seen the world disrupted by the bloodiest wars in recorded history, pointed out in both words and deeds, each according to his own temperament, the symbolic and practical function of the garden as a place of meditation and peace.

Both men looked closely at what was happening around them, but both saw beyond the immediate reality. Today, the idea that nature—and the garden, which is an interpretation of nature on a human scale—has a therapeutic value, both for the individual and for the society of which he is part, is a universally accepted fact. Science has adopted it by creating horticultural therapy, and politics by making the protection of the environment a concern of government.

In the homogenised society of our time, when the sense of personal identity is in danger of becoming lost, the care of plants and an awareness of the simplicity and rigour of the laws of nature can lead man back to an exploration, knowledge and acceptance of self. Gardening is an exercise in awareness. We have to get to know the plants and to understand their needs, to know how much time they will take to grow and how big they will be. We have to wait without becoming impatient and learn that nothing is permanent, that all things change, die and are reborn. Basically, gardening is an apprenticeship in love.

Love, in fact, is the next step that Hesse and Tagore invite us to take towards happiness. A love that, as we have said, should be understood as a disposition towards goodness and kindness, an ability to understand other people's situations, to make other people's suffering our own and share other people's joy. Hesse and Tagore adopted this disposition of the mind, along with a strong desire to educate—the former above all through his writings and his letters to a great many, often anonymous, correspondents, the latter with his school and university. Love is a prescription for happiness, one that each person can accomplish in his everyday behaviour, towards those close to him, and also more widely, through the many opportunities of voluntary work that have now an increasingly important place in our society. A number of recent studies on the influence of various human activities on mental health have confirmed the beneficial effect of acts of altruism on the person who performs them. According to Allan Luks, author of a popular book on this subject, *The Healing Power of Doing Good*, ninety per cent of those who work in the voluntary sector register above average mental health and superior reserves of energy.

The objection that spontaneously arises is that there are mental states that, in themselves, limit the possibility of taking positive action towards one's neighbours. Helping and loving others requires an optimistic vision of life and of oneself which the pessimist does not have and cannot create alone. What can help in such cases—and this is another idea that Hesse and Tagore have in common—is meditation and other practices based on control of the mind and body such as yoga. Hesse wrote often about meditation, long before it was widely practised in the West, and Tagore included it in the daily exercises of his school.

In the Laboratory for Affective Neuroscience at the University of Wisconsin, some interesting experiments have been conducted, with the use of tomography and magnetic resonance imaging, on the behaviour of the brain when the subject is experiencing strong emotions. The findings indicate that when we are happy the left side of the cerebral cortex is more active, and when we are sad, the right side. Richard J Davidson, the scientist in charge of the laboratory, has done experiments on Buddhist monks, recording the changes in brains during meditation, and registered a high quotient of activity on the left side—the side which, as we have seen, corresponds to a state of well-being. One of these monks was Matthieu Ricard, an interesting figure in his own right. Born in France immediately after the war, the son of a philosopher and a painter, and groomed for a promising career as a molecular biologist, Ricard grew dissatisfied with his life and, choosing the more rarefied path of spirituality, became a Buddhist monk. Intellectually close to the Dalai Lama, he is the author of several books, the latest of which is about happiness[98]—an inspiring research on the concept of happiness as found in various Eastern philosophical and religious traditions, seen through the mind and language of a European.

Logically speaking, meditation is the opposite of activity. It is stillness where activity is movement, it distracts thought from the surrounding reality whereas activity has reality as its object. And yet activity, when it does not occupy and submerge the thoughts of man but quietly submits to them, is just as important as meditation for a balanced life. The joy of little things and humble work well done can help us to forget ourselves, to drive away an obsession with our own image and the constant affirmation of the ego. If it then takes the form of creative activity, of whatever kind, it helps even more directly to liberate what is inside us. We do not need to be artists to be creative, nor do we need the praise or admiration of other people.

For many human beings, spirituality is linked to religion. Not that religious precepts are only concerned with the discipline of the spirit—in fact, they are as much about conduct as about thought. But for those who live in the shade of the great tree of the monotheistic religions, the meaning of man's life and destiny is contained in the dictates of faith. What both Hesse and Tagore urge us to do, implicitly in their works, in their poetry and fiction, is to separate religion and spirituality. Just as he has a physical life, so every human being has or should have a spiritual life, even though it may not necessarily be confined within the limits of a particular religious belief. The aspiration to transcendence may be expressed in a merging of different beliefs and traditions, or it may be the result of an individual, independent search. What matters, as far as man's freedom and happiness are concerned, is not just the observance of a dogma or obedience to a single teaching, but recognising a spiritual dimension in oneself and giving it free rein by submerging oneself in it, thereby coming to an understanding of the astonishing complexity of the world. The way of spirituality can sometimes be a long road to travel. It may require time and effort to learn about other doctrines, other cultures, other mystical experiences. Hesse had been brought up in a strict Pietistic environment and freeing himself from its rules certainly cost him a great deal of time and hard work. What helped him was his gradual assimilation of the Eastern culture of which he had had an inkling in his childhood. It is hard now to say which had the greatest influence on his thinking—Christianity, Buddhism or Taoism. Tagore, too, was familiar with different cultures, different religious strands, but asserted from an early age that his was a religion apart, "a poet's religion".

We cannot know everything that surrounds us, but we can learn to accept it. Beyond knowledge, there is tolerance towards what is strange, or even hostile to us. Hesse rejected his country when war forced its citizens to share in a general hatred for the enemy. Tagore distanced himself from those preaching the independence of India, even though he shared their aims, because it implied a feeling of hatred for the occupier. Both men believed that tolerance and the desire for peace were not only praiseworthy sentiments but an indispensable condition for being happy.

One of the biggest causes of suffering is fear. And the ultimate fear, the fear that worms its way into us in mid-life and will not let go of us, but grows and becomes stronger with time, is the fear of old age and death. It is a fear so old and so deep-rooted that every religion has devised an afterlife to minimise its effects and give us a reason to hope. Hesse and Tagore conquered this ancestral fear not with the promise of life after death, which would require a faith that cannot be learnt, but with a calm acceptance of the natural order, which encompasses good and evil, death and life, decay and regeneration.

Whether it is the patient reaching out to nature, the humble practice of everyday things, the various ways of art, the knowledge of other religions, the search for one's own religion, love for one's neighbour or love for all the things around us— each of these paths singly, and all of them combined, help us to find happiness. Neither Hesse nor Tagore wrote a breviary on how to become happy, they only indicated the path that every human being can take. It is the individual human being who is at the centre of life and it is from him that all roads start. Hesse wrote, in a letter to one of his many anguished correspondents, that life gives each person a unique and different task. Through self-knowledge, each person will discover their own path, find their own answer and, with it, their own share of happiness.

Notes

1 Katherine Mansfield *Bliss and Other Stories* London Bloomsbury Publishing 1994 p90.

2 Hermann Hesse *Happiness* (*Glück* 1949) GW VIII 480-491. The works of Hermann Hesse are quoted in the English translation or from the German edition: H Hesse *Gesammelte Werke* (12 voll) Frankfurt a M Suhrkamp 1970, indicated by the abbreviation GW.

3 Leo Tolstoy *Anna Karenina* translated by J Carmichael New York/Toronto/London Bantam books 1960 p1.

4 Hermann Hesse *Childhood of the Magician* (*Kindheit des Zauberers* 1923) GW VI p379.

5 Hermann Hesse *On Recent Novels* in *Die Propyläen* I 1904 p771-772.

6 Hermann Hesse *When it Is Evening* (*Wenn es Abend wird* 1904) from *Book of Images* (*Bilderbuch*) GW VI p182.

7 Hermann Hesse Letter of 6th April 1946 GW X p565.

8 Hermann Hesse *Demian* (*Demian* 1919) GW V p126.

9 Hermann Hesse *A Guest at the Spa* (*Kurgast* 1925) GW VII p112.

10 Hermann Hesse *Steppenwolf* (*Der Steppenwolf* 1927) GW VII p231.

11 Hermann Hesse Letter mid-March 1933 GWX p521.

12 Hermann Hesse *The Glass Bead Game* (*Das Glasperlenspiel* 1943) translated by C and R Winston London Vintage Books 2000 p298.

13 Hermann Hesse *Happiness* cit p13

14 Hermann Hesse *Peter Camenzind* (*Peter Camenzind* 1904) GWI p453.

15 Hermann Hesse *All Deaths* (*Alle Tode*) in HH *Poems* selected and translated by J Wright London Jonathan Cape 1971 p79.

16 Hermann Hesse *Peter Camenzind* cit p353

17 Hermann Hesse *Trees* (*Bäume* 1919) GW VI p151.

18 Ibid.

19 Hermann Hesse *Letters* (*Ausgewählte Briefe* ed by H and N Hesse Frankfurt aM Suhrkamp 2000).

20 Hermann Hesse *Peasant House* (*Bauernhaus* 1920) GW VI p133.

21 Hermann Hesse *The House of Dreams* (*Das Haus der Träume* 1920) in HH *Freude am Garten* ed by V Michels Frankfurt a M Insel 1992 pp159-188.

22 Hermann Hesse *Return to Spontaneity* (*Rückverwandlung* 1954) in *Freude am Garten* cit p133.

23 Hermann Hesse *Hours in the Garden (Stunden im Garten* 1936)
HH *Hours in the Garden and other Poems,* translated by R Lesser
London Jonathan Cape 1980 p47.

24 Rudolf Borchardt *The Passionate Gardener (Der leidenschaftliche
Gärtner)* Stuttgart Klett Cotta 1968.

25 Hermann Hesse *In the Garden (Im Garten* 1908) in *Freude am
Garten* cit p14.

26 Hermann Hesse *Lü Buwei Spring and Autumn (Lü Bu We
Frühling und Herbst)* GWXII p33.

27 Hermann Hesse *Childhood of the Magician* cit GW VI p376.

28 Hermann Hesse *A Library of World Literature (Eine Bibliothek der
Weltliteratur* 1929) GW XI p337.

29 Hermann Hesse *From India (Aus Indien* 1913) in *Aus Indien.
Aufzeichnungen Tagebücher Gedichte Betrachtungen und Erzählungen*
Frankfurt a M Suhrkamp 1980.

30 Hermann Hesse *The Journey to the East (Die Morgenlandfahrt*
1932). HH *The Journey to the East* translated by H Rosner
London Paladin Grafton Books 1989 p36.

31 Hermann Hesse *Bhagavad Gita* GWI p52.

32 Ibid.

33 Hermann Hesse *A Library of World Literature* cit GWXI p368.

34 Hermann Hesse letter to Romain Rolland 8th November
1921 in *Materialien zu Hermann Hesses Siddhartha* ed by V Michels
vol I Frankfurt a M Suhrkamp 1975 vol I p148.

35 Hermann Hesse *A Bit of Theology* (*Ein Stückchen Theologie* 1932) GW X pp74-88.

36 Hermann Hesse *A Guest at the Spa* cit GW VII 61.

37 Hermann Hesse Letter to Stefan Zweig 27th November 1922 in *Materialien zu Hermann Hesses Siddhartha* vol I cit p180.

38 Hermann Hesse *Siddhartha* cit p81.

39 Hermann Hesse Letter to a student 12th February 1950 in *Ausgewählte Briefe* cit

40 Hermann Hesse *Siddhartha* cit p111.

41 Hermann Hesse *The Glass Bead Game* cit p94.

42 Hermann Hesse *The Speeches of Buddha* (*Die Reden Buddhas* 1921) GWXII p21.

43 Hermann Hesse *Keyserling's Travel Diary* (*Reisetagebuch eines Philosophen* 1920) GW XII p468.

44 Carl G Jung *Yoga and the West* in CGJ *Collected Works vol XI Psychology and Religion: West and East* London Routledge & Kegan Paul 1958 pp529-608.

45 Hermann Hesse *My Belief* (*Mein Glaube* 1931) GWX p72.

46 Hermann Hesse *Siddhartha* cit p113.

47 Hermann Hesse *From the Diary of Martin* (*Aus Martins Tagebuch* 1918) in HH *Verstreute und kurze Prosa aus dem Nachlaß* ed by V Michels Frankfurt a M Suhrkamp 1977 pp132-133.

48 Hermann Hesse *A Guest at the Spa* cit p105-106.

49 Ibid.

50 Hermann Hesse *Gratitude to Goethe (Dank an Goethe 1932)*
GW XII p152.

51 Hermann Hesse Letter to Ina Seidel (Brief an Ina Seidel
12th September 1925) in HH *Gesammelte Briefe* vol II (1922-
1935) ed by U & V Michels Frankfurt a M Suhrkamp 1979
p120.

52 Hermann Hesse *Steppenwolf* cit GW VII p413.

53 Hermann Hesse *Maturity Makes us Young (Mit der Reife wird
man immer jünger* Frankfurt a M Insel 1990).

54 Hermann Hesse *Stages (Stufen* 1941) *The Glass Bead Game*
cit p421.

55 Krishna Kripalani *Rabindranath Tagore: A Biography*
Calcutta Visva-Bharati 1980 (2nd edn) p182.

56 Ibid p132-133.

57 Rabindranath Tagore *The Religion of Man* (1931) *The
English Writings of Rabindranath Tagore* ed by Sisir Kumar Das
vol III New Delhi Sahitya Academy
1996 p156.

58 See Krishna Dutta Andrew Robinson *Rabindranath Tagore:
the Myriad- Minded Man* London Bloomsbury 1995 pp67-77.

59 Edward Thompson *Rabindranath Tagore: Poet and Dramatist*
Calcutta 1979.

60 WB Yeats *Introduction to Rabindranath Tagore. Gitanjali: Song Offerings* (1912) in *The English Writings of Rabindranath Tagore* cit vol I p39.

61 Rabindranath Tagore *The Striving for Svaraj* in *Towards Universal Man* Bombay/London Asia Publishing House 1961 pp274-284.

62 Krishna Kripalani cit p284.

63 Rabindranath Tagore *A Flight of Swans* in *Poems from Balaka* translated by Aurobindo Bose London John Murray 1955 p93.

64 Ibid p21.

65 Rabindranath Tagore *Crisis in Civilization* in *The English Writings of Rabindranath Tagore* cit vol III p726.

66 Rabindranath Tagore *The Sun of the First Day* cit in K Dutta A Robinson op cit p367.

67 Rabindranath Tagore *The Message of the Forest* in *The English Writings of Sir Rabindranath Tagore* cit vol III pp385-400.

68 Rabindranath Tagore *Sadhana* (1913) in *The English Writings of Rabindranath Tagore* cit vol II p283.

69 Ibid.

70 Rabindranath Tagore *Flying Man* in *Selected Poems* translated by W Radice London Penguin books 1994 p113.

71 Rabindranath Tagore *My Reminiscences* (1917) Reprint Bibliobazar 2007 p172.

72 Ibid.

73 Rabindranath Tagore *Glimpses of Bengal Selected from the Letters of Rabindranath Tagore 1885 to 1895* (1921) Reprint Kessinger Publishing p70.

74 Rabindranath Tagore *In Praise of Trees* in *Selected Poems* cit p92.

75 Rabindranath Tagore *Gitanjali* cit p66.

76 Johann Wolfgang Goethe *Selige Sehnsucht* in *Poems of the West and East: West-Eastern Divan* translated by J Waley Bern Lang 1998.

77 Rabindranath Tagore *A Flight of Swans* cit pp63-64.

78 Rabindranath Tagore *Glimpses of Bengal* cit p32.

79 Rabindranath Tagore *The Religion of Man* cit pp120-128.

80 Rudyard Kipling *The Ballad of East and West* in *Rudyard Kipling Selected Verse* Harmondsworth 1977 p99.

81 Rabindranath Tagore *On the Eve of Departure* in *Towards Universal Man* cit pp158-174.

82 Ibid pp175-201.

83 Vivek Ranjan Bhattacharya *Tagore's Vision of a Global Family* New Delhi 1987 ppXI-XII.

84 Rabindranath Tagore *Brutal Night Comes Silently* in *Rabindranath Tagore: the Myriad-Minded Man* cit pp362-263.

85 Rabindranth Tagore *Sadhana* cit p325.

86 Ibid pp326-333.

87 Rabindranath Tagore *The Religion of Man* cit p169.

88 Rabindranath Tagore *What is Art?* in *Personality*, *The English Writings of Rabindranath Tagore* cit vol II pp347-416

89 Ibid.

90 Ibid p354.

91 Rabindranath Tagore *Sadhana* cit p336.

92 Rabrindanath Tagore *The Gardener* (1913) in *The English Writings of Rabindranath Tagore* cit vol I p.94.

93 Rabindranath Tagore *The Home and the World* (1919) translated by S Tagore London Penguin Books 2005 p50.

94 Cit in Martin Kämpchen *Rabindranath Tagore* Reinbek bei Hamburg Rororo 1992 p35.

95 Rabindranath Tagore Letter to Victoria Ocampo in *Rabindranath Tagore: an Anthology* New York St Martin's Griffin 1999 pp179-180.

96 Rabindranath Tagore *Sadhana* cit pp316-325.

97 Ibid.

98 Matthieu Ricard *Happiness: A Guide to Developing Life's Most Important Skill* New York/Boston Little, Brown and Company 2006.

ACKNOWLEDGEMENTS

Thanks go to Volker Michels, who knows absolutely everything about Hermann Hesse and is the editor of his *opera omnia*, to Regina Bucher, director of the Hesse Museum at Montagnola, to Mauro Ponzi, author of many studies of Hesse and tireless organiser of conferences, and to Eva Eberwein, who has brought Hesse's garden at Gaienhofen back to life.

I should also like to thank Irene Bignardi, who guided my first steps at Santiniketan, Martin Kämpchen for his time and help, and Mario Prayer, who, as a scholar of Tagore and of Indian history, carefully read the text and gave me some very helpful advice. A warm thank-you, too, to Melissa Ulfane of Pushkin Press, and, above all, to Boris Biancheri, without whose patience and intelligence the book would not have been written.